CW01668187

In and Around London by Rail

A guide to selected routes and towns

Jarrold Publishing, Norwich

CONTENTS

Front cover: A Liverpool Street to Cambridge train passing Bethnal Green

Back cover: St Pancras Station

Title page: Dwarfed by the City skyline, a Thameslink train crosses Blackfriars Bridge (*Photo:* Ray King)

Opposite: St Stephen's Tower, which houses Big Ben, Palace of Westminster (*Photo:* H. Atkinson)

INTRODUCTION

In and Around London by Rail is one of a series of books compiled by the Railway Development Society, a body which aims to represent the interests of all rail users. The London area is well served by a comprehensive rail network and in this volume we invite you to go exploring by train, for within this diverse and cosmopolitan region lies a wealth of interest which, as we hope to show, is easily accessible by public transport.

Unfortunately, a book of this size must necessarily be selective and we have tended to focus on suburban rather than central London, although the net has been cast wide, as a glance at the list of contents will show. The abbreviations (L) and (R) have been used to indicate whether features are to the left or right as seen from a train when facing the direction of travel.

Although this book is written with the general reader, rather than the railway enthusiast, in mind, it may be worthwhile to consider briefly some background information. The railways were owned and operated by many independent companies until 1923, when they were amalgamated into four major concerns. Among the few railways excluded from this grouping were the Underground lines in London, most of which (together with the London General Omnibus Company) were controlled by the Underground Electric Railways. In 1933 this company's interests, and the Metropolitan Railway, were brought under the unified control of a newly created London Transport Executive, usually referred to simply as London Transport. In 1948 LTE and the 'Big Four' railways – Great Western, London Midland & Scottish, London & North Eastern, and Southern – were nationalised, merging to form British Railways.

Although the Underground is popularly known as 'the tube', this term should, strictly, be confined to the deep-level (Bakerloo, Central, Jubilee, Northern, Piccadilly and Victoria) lines which burrow their way beneath the city in small-diameter tunnels or 'tubes'. Even the term 'Underground' is something of a misnomer, since the greater part of the system is, in fact, above ground.

Recently the activities of both BR and LT have been split into separate business sectors, probably with the ultimate objective of denationalisation. Services on the local railways featured in this book are provided by two undertakings: the Network SouthEast sector of British Rail, and London Underground Limited together with its wholly-owned subsidiary Docklands Light Railway. The latter are part of London Regional Transport which has overall responsibility for London's Underground and bus services.

Use of specialist terminology has as far as possible been avoided but the following information may be of interest. Many of the trains which you are likely to encounter will consist of coaches which are not hauled by a locomotive: these are multiple units, either electric (emu) or diesel (dmu). Electric trains draw their power from overhead wires, or from a third (conductor) rail alongside the track, in each case current returning via the wheels and running rails to complete a circuit. On lines used by Underground services the current returns instead through a fourth (negative) rail laid along the centre of the track. On BR lines, trains travelling towards London are referred to as 'up' services whilst those in the opposite direction are 'down' trains. On the London Underground, where such distinctions are less relevant, trains are northbound, southbound, eastbound or westbound, according to the general direction of travel, and this information is used extensively on station signs.

For up-to-date details of reduced fares, including the popular one-day Travelcard, please consult your nearest staffed station. You may also find the free NSE leaflets 'Your Guide to Travel in Network SouthEast' and 'Leisure Travel Guide' helpful, and useful free guides to Underground fares and tickets are also available from LRT stations, and enquiry offices at Heathrow, King's Cross, St James's Park, Oxford Circus, Piccadilly Circus and Victoria stations. Both BR and LRT issue free maps and timetable leaflets; BR also publishes local booklets, for which a small charge is made, as well as a complete national timetable.

Train services are subject to alteration; the information in this book, generally based on off-peak patterns at the time of writing, is intended for guidance only. Services tend to be varied at busy periods, and essential maintenance work sometimes has to be carried out, often at weekends, which may result in delays and diversions.

Please avoid travel during Monday to Friday rush hours (approximately 7.30 a.m. to 9.30 a.m. and 4.30 p.m. to 6.30 p.m.) if you possibly can. Trains tend to be extremely busy then, and by avoiding these times you can probably take advantage of cheaper fares. Smoking is prohibited throughout the Underground, both at stations and on trains, a ban which is likely to be extended soon to some NSE services.

Always verify in advance opening times of places you wish to visit. Please see the Further Information pages for useful addresses, and more details about buses, also taking cycles by train.

Every editor relies upon the knowledge and expertise of others, and I am greatly indebted to each of the contributors. Any mistakes are probably the result of my additions and amendments rather than the work of the original authors. Lastly, thanks are due to my wife for her tolerance and invaluable help in preparing the text.

Ian McGill
Westbury, Wiltshire
June 1990

An Island Gardens to Stratford train approaches All Saints station on the Docklands Light Railway (*Photo:* John C. Baker)

WINDSOR CIRCULAR

by Ian McGill

Windsor is served by two rail routes from London; thus one may travel either from Paddington, changing trains at Slough, or from Waterloo direct at half-hourly intervals (hourly on Sundays). Frequent local and InterCity trains calling at Slough connect with a half-hourly branch line service which runs daily to Windsor & Eton Central, and the journey from Paddington can sometimes take only thirty minutes, whilst through trains from Waterloo to Windsor & Eton Riverside take about forty-seven minutes. Passengers using Paddington should be guided by the train departure indicators or station announcements when seeking the correct platform. At Waterloo the train will almost invariably leave from the group of platforms numbered 16 to 21, often referred to as 'the Windsor side' of the station.

With termini on two different lines, Windsor lends itself as the focal point of a circular trip and this chapter has been arranged accordingly, starting at Paddington and ending at Waterloo, in anticipation of providing added interest.

The district around Paddington was planned and laid out as a residential area early last century. St Mary's Hospital, where Sir Alexander Fleming made his discovery of the drug penicillin, is almost next door to the present main line terminus of the former Great Western Railway. Occupying thirteen acres, this station, which dates from 1854, is largely hidden from Praed Street by the Great Western Royal Hotel, the work of P. C. Hardwick, who also designed Euston's Great Hall. The magnificent overall roof, although extended in 1916, remains substantially the work of the eminent Victorian engineer Isambard Kingdom Brunel and his associate Matthew Digby Wyatt, who were influenced in their design by Paxton's Crystal Palace. From a commanding position at the head of a flight of stairs leading to the Circle and District Underground lines, John Doubleday's sculpture of Brunel looks out across a busy concourse known as 'The Lawn', because it is variously supposed to have been occupied by cottage gardens or a grassy slope separating Praed Street from the original station of 1838. Alongside platform 1 the former royal waiting room can be identified by a doorway over which appear a crown and the GWR armorial device; further along but high above, a fine oriel window gave the company's directors a panoramic view across the station from their boardroom. The GWR war memorial commemorates those employees who gave their lives fighting in two World Wars.

To the right of the Bakerloo Line entrance and facing the cab road an insignificant gated opening, unnoticed by most people, leads to the Post Office Railway, an underground line opened in 1927 which is devoted exclusively to carrying mail between Paddington and Eastern District Office, serving Liverpool Street and main post offices *en route*. Paddington Bear, who is much more widely known and appreciated, stands encapsulated in glass on The Lawn, a reminder that the London Toy and Model Museum is in nearby Craven Hill (tel. 071 262 7905/9450), occupying a pair of Victorian houses to provide almost limitless interest, including outdoor activities in the garden, for children of all ages. In the future, Paddington station is destined to assume a major role in international travel with the advent of an electrified surface rail link to Heathrow Airport.

Threading its way out of **Paddington**, our train is at first accompanied (R) by the elevated A40 motorway and the Hammersmith branch of the Metropolitan Line, which having emerged alongside platforms 15 and 16 from its subterranean wanderings, soon pauses at Royal Oak station (R), before diving under the main lines at Subway Junction and reappearing (L) at **Westbourne Park**. Here, Metropolitan trains veer away southwards in tandem with the A40(M) which stalks across our path, providing sanctuary for a London Buses garage (R), crouching cat-like beneath the concrete spans. Tower blocks vie for attention with flats on a more human scale which cower subserviently at their feet, and as the train hurries past Kensal Green carriage servicing plant (R) there is a brief glimpse of Kensal Green Cemetery. Massive girder bridges carry Scrubs Lane and the West London Line overhead, across a broad expanse of tracks which fan out (R) into Old Oak carriage sidings.

A massive retaining wall skirting the depot keeps the Grand Union Canal at bay. The towpath provides an unparalleled view of railway activities below, and opposite the urban veil retreats like an autumnal mist to reveal the broad expanse of Wormwood Scrubs, devoid of trees save around its edges, because it was once an RAF station. Beyond lies the grim and unmistakable outline of the prison, which was built by convict labour. The old GWR main line to Birmingham diverges (R) close to Old Oak High Speed Train depot and there is a panoramic view (L) over the irregular west London skyline as we pass, in quick succession, above the Central Line and under the North London Line (page 29). From this route a spur descends behind **Acton (Main Line)** station to the remnants of Acton yard beyond, where private sidings (R) serve the premises of Messrs. Redland, and a Foster Yeoman aggregate depot.

Acton is served by seven stations bearing its title, four of them named from the cardinal points of the compass. Well House Road, near North Acton station (Central Line) recalls the existence of Acton Wells, which enjoyed a brief period of popularity in the eighteenth century, its saline waters attracting visitors from London. In 1870 a German biergarten was established on the site, which survived until the First World War. A branch of the Central Line runs alongside (R), joined by District Line trains at **Ealing Broadway**, where Underground services terminate.

Situated opposite Haven Green, the station is convenient for the excellent facilities of this suburb. Pitshanger Manor museum in Mattock Lane shows the work of architect Sir John Soane. Demand for building space has resulted in development above the railway, which runs in a covered way towards **West Ealing**, where the bustling shopping area is just to the south along Uxbridge Road. A single line sneaks away (R) to Greenford, skirting as it does so the works of Plasser, manufacturers of sophisticated on-track railway maintenance machines. An area of large villas is interrupted by leafy Kensington Cemetery (L) and a westward-facing spur from the Greenford line trails in (R), approaching **Hanwell & Elthorne**.

The 'down' main platform has been removed, and much of the remainder of the station might well have suffered demolition but for timely local intervention; instead the station has been beautifully restored and is a splendid example of what can be achieved with a more positive approach. Almost at once the suburban streets recede and trains are borne aloft on the graceful Wharncliffe Viaduct, an eight-arched masonry structure named after Lord Wharncliffe, who was instrumental in the successful passage through Parliament of the first GWR Bill, and whose armorial device is incorporated above the centre pier. Distant Harrow-on-the-Hill rises nobly from the landscape (R) while below, Church Fields slope gently to the River Brent.

Sheltered by the trees of Brent Lodge Park, Hanwell church (R) is the burial place of Jonas Hanway who some 240 years ago braved contemporary ridicule when he introduced us to the novel idea of umbrellas. Across busy Uxbridge Road, a continuation, albeit far removed, of London's busy Oxford Street shopping thoroughfare, the site of the former AEC motor works, where many of London's buses were built, lies alongside (L) awaiting redevelopment. The initials AEC signified Associated Equipment Company, which started life as the former London General Omnibus Company's vehicle manufacturing division.

At **Southall** station a branch, long since closed to passenger trains but still busy with freight, trails in (L) from Brentford. A short distance away at Windmill Bridge three transport modes intersect, crossing each other simultaneously at different levels, Windmill Road at the highest level bridging the Grand Union Canal which in turn spans the Brentford branch railway. This interesting site may be reached on foot via Park Avenue, Glade Lane and the canal towpath. The tall, battlemented octagonal building (R) began life as a water-tower but has recently been converted to flats. A vast expanse of stored cars (R) marks the site of Southall Gasworks, of which the manufacturing capacity was rendered redundant with the advent of North Sea gas supplies.

The next few miles are characterised by an industrial presence largely developed on the initiative of the GWR which, anxious to tap potential sources of freight revenue, offered attractive incentives to firms willing to locate here and use the company's goods facilities. Two arms of the Grand Union Canal are crossed in succession, and there is a private siding (R) which receives aggregates traffic. Nestle's factory adjoins the railway (L) at **Hayes & Harlington**, and other premises include the extensive Thorn/EMI works (R). London's major international airport at Heathrow lies less than two miles south, evidenced by the increasing frequency of low flying aircraft. Another aggregate terminal which receives block train loads of stone (R) is on the approach to **West Drayton**, where a single track meandering shyly behind the rail-connected coal concentration depot (R) used to fork, north to serve Uxbridge and south to Staines; only a truncated portion of the latter now survives, for goods, passing under the main line west of the station.

Crossing the River Colne, trains pass briefly into Buckinghamshire through an area pock-marked with the scars of gravel extraction to reach **Iver**. A 1920s red-brick shopping parade adjoins an unpretentious station, opened between the two World Wars to serve the then new Richings Park estate, but the original settlement, with a sixteenth-century inn and a church containing Saxon and Norman work, is three-quarters of a mile north. Coppins, a nineteenth-century house, was for many years occupied by the Duke of Kent and Princess Marina. Traversing scruffy urban fringe country, a rail-served oil terminal (R) adjoins **Langley** station, but the former Ford motor plant (L) has been demolished. Langley is an unpromising place, but its church is lavishly endowed with fine monuments and furnishings, mostly through the generosity of previous owners of Langley Park. The present house was built 250 years ago for the third Duke of Marlborough who found Blenheim Palace too remote from London. Langley Park has been incorporated into the linear Colne Valley Park which stretches from Rickmansworth to Staines. Keep looking in this direction and you will probably get a first distant glimpse of Windsor Castle, in Royal Berkshire, as the train hurries towards **Slough**.

Alight here and proceed to platform 1 for the brief journey by diesel multiple unit to Windsor. There is little of interest at Slough to detain casual visitors, except to note that it is the western outpost of London's red buses (route 81 from Hounslow) and the nearest station to Stoke Poges, a village about a mile distant which is associated with the poem *Elegy in a Country Churchyard* by Thomas Gray, whose mortal remains were laid to rest there. Pioneer astronomer William Herschel, who in 1781 discovered the planet Uranus, carried out much of his work at Slough. The present Observatory House occupies the site of his former home. Salt Hill was so called because it was here that boys from Eton College sold salt to raise funds for university expenses. Flags were given in return for purchases, and thus the idea for charity flag days was born.

The Eton College authorities at first succeeded in keeping railways out of Windsor, and until 1849 Slough offered the nearest approach by train. Indeed, the first royal journey by train began at Slough when on 13 June 1842 Queen Victoria and Prince Albert set out by rail for Paddington.

The GWR was a pioneer bus operator and Slough became the focal point of a network of local 'road motor' services, as the company rather quaintly referred to them, as well as the main overhaul centre for its vehicle fleet. The Horlicks factory,

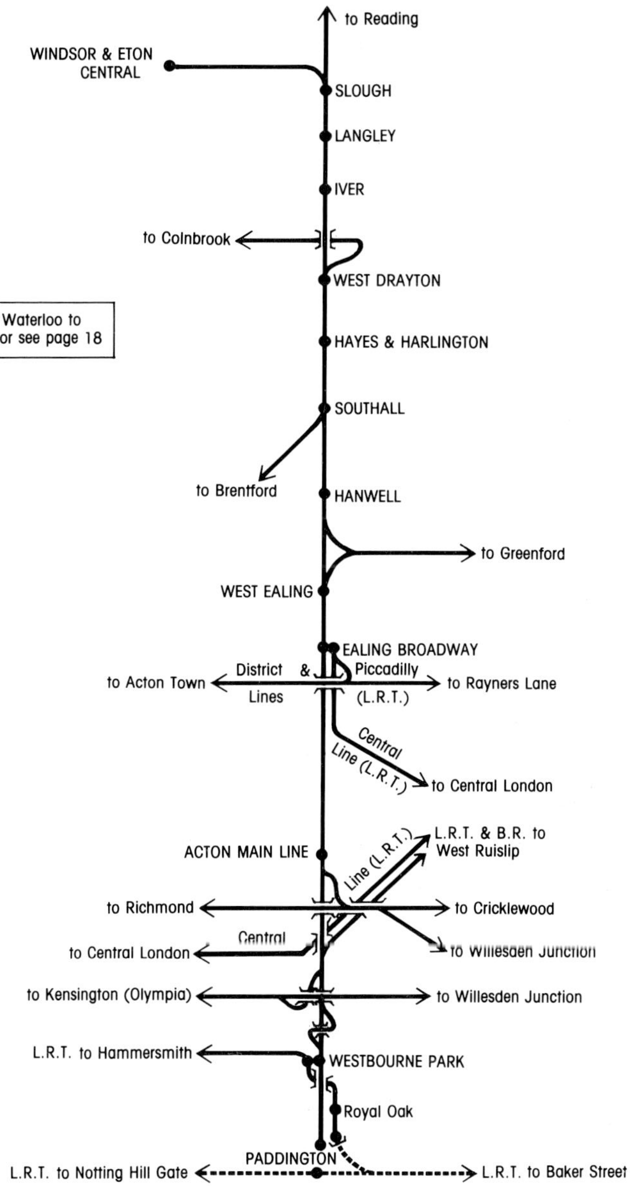

modelled on parent premises in America, is a fortress-like building of 1908 glimpsed (R) as Windsor trains turn away from the main line immediately beyond Slough station.

Shortly the overgrown remains of a spur come in (R) from the west. Known unofficially as the 'Royal Curve' on account of frequent use by the royal train, the spur also enabled other trains to gain access to Windsor from the rest of the network, but it was removed more than twenty-five years ago when the branch was reduced to a basic single-track railway, since when special services to the town from elsewhere on the system have had to make a long detour to use Riverside station. Travelling mostly on embankment and viaduct, trains offer a fine panorama of the surrounding scene which has, unfortunately, been spoiled in recent years by unsightly development and new roads. There are no intermediate stations along the branch, although a short-lived halt was once provided at Chalvey Road to serve Upton-by-Chalvey, a village which has been engulfed by Slough but which is a rival claimant for the setting of Gray's *Elegy*.

Eton lies spread out below (L) and passing close to Windsor racecourse our train makes a cautious approach to the River Thames on a long curving viaduct, as if anxious to avoid crossing. Finally, realising that there is no choice but to bridge the water, it does so in style, by means of a 200-foot-span wrought iron bridge, to reach **Windsor & Eton Central** station. The terminus is well named, situated in the very heart of Windsor and opposite the castle.

Since 1968 only one of the four platforms has been used; in 1983 Madame Tussaud's took over the remaining platform space to stage a special exhibition commemorating the 1897 Diamond Jubilee of Queen Victoria's accession to the throne. Currently known as 'Royalty and Empire', this superb and colourful spectacle is open daily (except Christmas Day) and incorporates the original royal waiting room, which has been carefully restored to its former glory (tel. 0753 857837).

Royal Windsor is dominated by the magnificent castle, seat of British sovereigns for nine centuries, and the largest inhabited castle in the world. This huge complex occupies some thirteen acres and includes work spanning virtually every period since the Norman Conquest over 900 years ago. Several areas may be visited, including the royal apartments which are still regularly used by the royal family. Many varied exhibits are on view within the castle, but as opening times and admission charges may vary it is advisable to check by telephoning 0753 831118. St George's Chapel, dominating the castle precincts, contains the banners and insignia of the Order of the Garter as well as the remains of ten monarchs who were buried within its walls. Home Park includes the Royal Mausoleum at Frogmore, where Queen Victoria and her consort Prince Albert were laid to rest. Visitors are, however, only permitted on rare occasions.

Before the Norman invaders made their stronghold in the parish of Clewer, on the site of the present castle, Saxon kings had earlier built a residence, now all but vanished, some two miles distant near the village which has since become known as Old Windsor. Here you will find the uniquely-named pub The Bells of Ouzeley. Ouzeley is a corruption of Osney, near Oxford, where there was once an abbey noted for its particularly fine peal of bells, though quite why this should be remembered here is not entirely clear.

Windsor Great Park covers a vast area and includes some outstandingly beautiful gardens where countless species of flowering plants and shrubs may be admired. Animal and bird life flourishes here too; deer wander freely and large numbers of waterfowl may be seen at Virginia Water. This extensive artificial lake lies towards the southern extremity of the park and is about 1½ miles from Virginia Water station (page 20).

Windsor is a pleasant town, to which an excellent introduction is provided by frequent open-top bus tours. The fine parish church is complemented by an abundance of elegant Georgian and Victorian architecture and there is a superb selection of shops. Pause to see the Guildhall, and notice how the columns soaring upwards do not quite reach the roof and offer no support, having been added for aesthetic reasons rather than through structural necessity.

At Windsor Safari Park, ten minutes away by bus, there is the chance to meet many

Windsor Castle, from Alexandra Gardens

creatures from the animal kingdom almost face-to-face. Stroll across traffic-free Windsor Bridge and you are in neighbouring Eton, with its antique shops. Eton College is a celebrated public school founded in 1440 by King Henry VI. When the railway finally reached Windsor, the college was so concerned that its presence might endanger the moral welfare of the school that a ten-foot-high wall was built to screen it from the pupils' gaze. The Eton 'Wall Game' is a strange variant of rugby football which has its own rules and is played annually on St Andrew's Day (30 November) between the Collegers (who live in), and the Oppidans (who board in the town). Two miles west of Slough and an easy cycle ride along the B3026, Dorney Court is the perfect example of a Tudor manor house. Dating from about 1440, its time mellowed walls of brick and timber exude an atmosphere of history made tangible by the superb oak and exquisite furnishings within. In summer you can pick fresh soft fruit and eat delicious home-made cream teas. For opening arrangements telephone Burnham (Bucks) 0628 604638.

Leisurely river trips are a splendid way to observe the scenery, and facilities are available from the landing stages close to Windsor Bridge and alongside Riverside station. If you have time to spare, it is possible to take a trip upstream to Maidenhead, Marlow or Henley (see *Thames and Downs by Rail*), returning thence to Paddington by train.

Electric trains for Waterloo depart from **Windsor & Eton Riverside** station beside the Thames in Datchet Road, close to Windsor Bridge and a short distance downhill from the town centre. Riverside was the terminus of the London & South Western Railway, which reached Datchet in 1848, but like its arch-rival the Great Western Railway was unable to gain access to Windsor until 1849. To do so it had to cross part of Home Park, and the money paid to the Crown for this privilege was used to make improvements at Windsor Castle. Electric train services commenced in 1930. Altogether a more intimate, homely affair than its rather pompous and overbearing neighbour, the attractive Tudor style of Riverside station is not lacking in dignity, and there are several features worth noting. Arched openings in the wall flanking Datchet Road were intended to facilitate access for cavalry travelling by train. At intervals along this wall the initials VR and PA, signifying Queen Victoria and her husband Prince Albert, appear in black bricks; the former royal waiting room is at the London end of the station. The bell-turret of this building was reputedly used as a look-out so that station staff could be alerted to the approach of royalty.

Setting out beside the river (L), with Eton huddled along its opposite bank and the Home Park (R) for company, we soon cross the Thames to reach **Datchet**. The river meanders alongside (R), with Old Windsor beyond, as our train approaches **Sunnymeads** along a three-mile stretch of straight track between Datchet and Staines. Numerous branches of the River Colne are encountered, tarrying among worked-out gravel pits before reluctantly joining Old Father Thames on his way to the sea. Runnymede, with its RAF memorial on Coopers Hill, and the Kennedy Freedom Memorial are away to the right, near Magna Charta Island, but as there is no river crossing in the vicinity the approach for rail passengers is by way of Egham station (page 19).

Leaving **Wraysbury** station beside the massive grass-covered earthworks of Wraysbury Reservoir, where Berkshire meets Surrey, Moor Lane soon swings overhead and a spur strikes out to serve Staines West Oil Terminal, at the severed end of a branch first encountered on the outward journey at West Drayton.

After crossing the busy High Street, Reading and Chertsey line trains converge (R) at **Staines**, which together with the remainder of the route to Waterloo is featured more fully on pages 15–19. Beyond **Ashford** a Borstal institution adjoins the railway (R) and we are within 1½ miles of Heathrow Airport. Consideration was once given to providing a surface railway across the largely unbuilt-on area of land (L) near **Feltham**, but this proposal was eventually rejected in favour of a tube link which was achieved by projecting the Piccadilly Line west from Hounslow. Heavy cross-London goods traffic used to be handled at Feltham marshalling yard beyond the station (R) until it was closed following a reappraisal of freight facilities during the 1960s. Hounslow Loop services (page 16) diverge at a triangular junction (L), but trains on the main route continue via **Whitton**, to be joined at **Twickenham**, home of English rugby football, by a loop from New Malden on the Waterloo–Woking main line (page 25).

After **St Margarets** station the train crosses the Thames in company with Twickenham road bridge (L) to reach **Richmond**, where connections may be made with District and North London Line trains (page 29), which diverge (L) before **North Sheen** station, opened in 1930. **Mortlake**, once famed for tapestry production, is the finishing point of the annual Oxford and Cambridge boat race; at **Barnes** the Hounslow Loop returns (L) from its perambulations around Brentford and Isleworth. A viaduct at **Putney** carries the Wimbledon branch of the District Line high above and a connection descends to join our route at Point Pleasant Junction, near **Wandsworth Town**. A maze of lines eagerly converging upon London meet at **Clapham Junction** as the suburban landscape gives way to a city skyline dominated by high-rise buildings. **Queenstown Road (Battersea)**, surrounded by tenements and hemmed in by a tangled web of railways heading single-mindedly towards Victoria, is only a short walk from Battersea Park (page 15).

The New Covent Garden Market (R) stands opposite the site of Nine Elms terminus, which became a goods depot after being superseded as a passenger station in 1848 by Waterloo. As the train weaves a curvaceous path through canyons of towering office blocks, there are tantalising glimpses of the Thames near **Vauxhall**, with Lambeth Palace, residence of the Archbishop of Canterbury (L), and views of the Tate Gallery and Houses of Parliament along the final approach to **Waterloo**.

SOUTH-WEST LONDON I: THE CITY, AND WATERLOO TO WOKING AND WEYBRIDGE VIA HOUNSLOW AND RICHMOND

by Alex Johnson and Ian McGill

Lacking both the historic grandeur and the modern functional ugliness of some other London termini, Waterloo is a bright business-like complex, its spacious uncluttered concourse sweeping in a broad scimitar curve behind twenty-one platforms. For the statistically minded, to this total may be added four further platforms at Waterloo (East) served by trains from Charing Cross, two platforms for BR's only tube railway (the Waterloo & City Line), and four London Regional Transport platforms for the Bakerloo and Northern Underground lines, giving a total of thirty-one in all.

Officially opened by Queen Mary in 1922, the present terminus was the result of a twelve-year rebuilding programme to replace a confusing conglomeration which had evolved from the original station of 1848 to serve the London & South Western Railway's complex main line and suburban network. With construction of the Channel Tunnel under way and the prospect of through trains to Europe, it is now poised on the brink of a new era as an international rail terminal.

The Waterloo & City Line, often known as 'The Drain', resulted from the LSWR's wish to reach the City of London, and since a surface railway was impractical the only alternative was to go below ground. Thus in 1898 a 1½-mile tube link of its own was opened between Waterloo and the station now known as Bank (City), where access to LRT Underground services is provided by a 302-foot travolator or 'moving pavement', which was something of a novelty when installed some thirty years ago. There are no intermediate stations, and frequent services taking five minutes for the journey operate until shortly after 9.30 p.m. Mondays to Fridays and lunchtime on Saturdays. There are no Sunday trains. One of the oldest tube railways, the Waterloo & City was the first to adopt multiple unit trains. The present rolling stock, which is about to be replaced, dates from 1940, and as there is no physical connection with the rest of the railway system coaches have to be brought to the surface by means of hoists, one of which is located beyond platform 21 at Waterloo.

Bank station is, as the name suggests, close to the Bank of England, which is often popularly referred to as 'The Old Lady of Threadneedle Street'. Bankers to the Government and custodian of the nation's gold reserves, the Bank of England was incorporated by Royal Charter in 1694 to finance a conflict with France. During the anti-Catholic Gordon Riots of 1780 the bank came under threat, since when a military guard has been posted at the premises every night. The original buildings, designed by Sir John Soane, were extensively altered before the outbreak of war in 1939. The Bank of England Museum, open daily (free), provides a unique insight into this famous financial institution. Nearby is the Stock Exchange, first formed in 1801, and the Mansion House, built between 1739 and 1753 as official residence of the Lord Mayor of London. A little further afield, St Paul's Cathedral (page 45) can be reached on foot by way of Cheapside. Alternatively, an escalator connection with Monument station (Circle and District lines) enables one to visit the 202-foot-high Monument, a fluted Doric column of 1677 by Sir Christopher Wren commemorating the Great Fire of London in 1666, which began at a shop nearby in Pudding Lane. Crowned by a golden flame, the Monument has 311 steps which ascend within the pillar to reach a balcony which commands excellent views of London.

At **Waterloo**, the effect of the huge and imposing Victory Arch entrance forming the LSWR war memorial is, unfortunately, somewhat diminished by the proximity of a viaduct carrying trains to and from Charing Cross (page 76). Lower down the cab

Left: The Monument (*Photo:* H. Atkinson). Right: The Bank of England

road (L) notice a monumental lion, originally a trade mark of the defunct Lion Brewery, and which stood on the south bank of the Thames until moved here in 1951. It was made locally in 1837 from Coade Stone, a very durable artificial material whose formula has since been lost. Coade Stone sculptures are found elsewhere in London, most commonly in the form of 'Charity Children', figures of boys and girls adorning the façades of former Charity Schools, which educated children who would otherwise have been denied the benefit of tutoring in the days before free state schools. At its south bank end Waterloo Bridge, rebuilt in 1939, is flanked by the National Theatre and the Queen Elizabeth and Royal Festival Halls, which provide venues for numerous cultural events, and further south along Waterloo Road stands the Old Vic Theatre. Florence Nightingale founded the first school of nursing in 1860 at St Thomas's Hospital, and it is therefore fitting that on the site in Lambeth Palace Road a museum devoted to the life and work of this remarkable woman has been established (tel. 071 620 0374). A bridge spanning Waterloo Road between the terminus and East stations was built to carry a single-track connection between the two, but it was little used and now provides covered pedestrian access.

Hounslow Loop stations have a half-hourly train service on weekdays (hourly on Sundays), most of which continue to Woking (Weybridge at peak times and on Sundays) via Staines and Chertsey, normally calling at all stations. Richmond is on a more direct route to Staines, which is served by trains to Reading, Windsor, and Guildford via Ascot, providing up to five trains each hour (two on Sundays), but the stopping pattern *en route* varies. Two additional trains each hour (one on Sundays) call at stations to Twickenham before branching off to Kingston.

These services usually depart from platforms 16 to 21, and looking back (R) as the train sets out, one can see the huge Shell Centre towering awesomely over a vast web of shining steel which emerges from Waterloo station, quickly converging to become eight tracks snaking on a viaduct among the tall buildings of Lambeth, Vauxhall and Battersea. Almost at once Westminster Bridge Road passes beneath, and sidings (L) mark the site of the London Necropolis Company's private station, destroyed during a wartime air raid, and from which funeral trains ran to Brookwood Cemetery, near Woking. During the next few minutes there are intermittent glimpses (R) of the Houses of Parliament across the Thames, dominated by Big Ben (page 77), before trains skirt Archbishops Park, the setting for Lambeth Palace, official residence of the Archbishop of Canterbury.

Milk traffic from the West Country used to be received by rail at **Vauxhall** station, an interchange with Victoria Line Underground services. Vauxhall Bridge, rebuilt in 1906, was the first in London to carry trams and replaced a structure known as Regent Bridge in honour of the future King George IV. Its design features a series of figures, Greek goddesses personifying the Arts and Sciences, who stare transfixed upon the waters below, each clasping an appropriate artefact: Architecture, for example, holds a model of St Paul's Cathedral. Vauxhall Gardens were a popular pleasure resort until the middle of the last century; firework displays were a favourite feature there. Cricket has been played since 1845 at Kennington Oval, home of Surrey County Cricket Club, which also staged early FA Cup Final football matches. Although Oval Underground station (Northern Line) is rather closer, the ground is only a short walk from Vauxhall via Harleyford Road. Nine Elms, superseded as a passenger terminus in 1848 by Waterloo, occupied a now redeveloped riverside site (R), opposite the New Covent Garden Market (L). Battersea Power Station, now closed and being transformed into a major leisure complex, rears above the rooftops (R), a familiar feature of the skyline for over fifty years.

A maze of lines converging in wild confusion upon Victoria station pass over and under our route in the vicinity of **Queenstown Road (Battersea)** station, which has platforms only on the Windsor and Reading lines. Battersea Park is close by, with an entrance opposite Battersea Park station, and was created in 1856/7 by dumping spoil from the Royal Victoria Dock site in east London (page 65) at Battersea Fields, where in 1829 the Duke of Wellington fought a duel with the Earl of Winchilsea. Battersea Dogs' Home, refuge for London's stray canines, is also nearby, accommodated in arches beneath the viaduct approaches to Victoria.

A multitude of tracks converge upon **Clapham Junction**, Britain's busiest station, which has recently received much needed improvements in connection with a major shopping development. Parting company with routes to the south and west which sweep away (L), our train calls at the low-numbered Windsor and Reading line platforms, separated by carriage sidings from the rest of the station. Continuing by way of **Wandsworth Town**, the train encounters the River Wandle close to its confluence with the Thames (R) where the historic Surrey Iron Railway terminated. Authorised in 1801 and opened to Croydon and Hackbridge in 1803, this plateway was the first public railway to be sanctioned by Parliament, and the earliest in the London area. Motive power was provided by horses, which, like the wagons, were supplied by customers who paid a toll to use the line. Receipts were disappointing and within half a century it had closed, but parts of the route were later used by conventional railways. Wandsworth's new museum (tel. 081 871 7074) portrays the history of this Thamesside area, the water-powered industries of the Wandle, and the transformation from country to suburbia.

Looking at the murky Wandle today, it is difficult to imagine that Izaak Walton (of *Compleat Angler* fame) and John Evelyn, the diarist, could enthuse over its virtues as a trout stream. A long-forgotten route to Wimbledon diverges at Point Pleasant

Junction to join the District Line which stalks across our way on a lofty viaduct at **Putney**. From 1888 until the advent of the Greater London Council eighty years later, this was where suburban Surrey, already in retreat, merged with an advancing metropolis. More tangible interest is provided by the annual inter-varsity boat race between rowing eights from Oxford and Cambridge, who compete each spring over a course from Putney to Mortlake. At **Barnes** the Hounslow Loop leaves the direct line to Staines – the description of the direct line continues on page 17.

The loop line is bounded by Barnes Common and Barn Elms Park (R) before reaching **Barnes Bridge** station. Weatherboard cottages and Georgian houses at Barnes Terrace gaze wistfully across the Thames; on boat race day special trains used to be stopped on the bridge to enable spectators to obtain a grandstand view of the event. **Chiswick** is the station for Chiswick House, a Palladian-style villa built in 1727 for the 3rd Earl of Burlington to house his library and collections of paintings. A temple, conservatory and canal are major visual focal points of the grounds, which also contain some interesting statuary. Open at various times (tel. 081 995 0508), Chiswick House should be approached via Burlington Lane. In Church Street, pause to admire the parish church of St Nicholas, which has fabric dating back to 1450, before going on to discover Chiswick Mall, where a variety of building styles spanning almost 400 years vie for attention. A Queen Anne style house in Hogarth Lane was the country retreat of painter William Hogarth (1697–1764) and contains an exhibition of his work which may be visited at certain times (tel. 081 994 6757).

Shortly after leaving Chiswick there is a level-crossing with Grove Park Terrace, where three houses, numbers 62 to 66, were bought by the LSWR, which demolished the middle one to make room for the railway. Passing beneath tracks used by District and North London Line services, our train arrives at **Kew Bridge**, where it was once possible to join London, Midland & Scottish Railway electric trains for north London. A favourite haunt of artists, Strand-on-the-Green (or, more correctly, Strand-on-Green) is a picturesque medley of cottages and houses whose walls, separated only by a path from the river, are covered by trailing plants which bloom in a summertime profusion of colour. Across the water at Kew Green, where St Anne's Church (1714) has associations with King George III, are some fine eighteenth-century houses adjoining Kew Gardens. An alternative approach is possible via Kew Gardens station (page 30).

North from Kew Bridge station, beyond the ugly M4 viaduct, Gunnersbury House, in a parkland setting, dates from 1801–2 and was the home of the Rothschild family. Now a local history museum it houses a varied and extensive collection of exhibits relating to Ealing and Hounslow (tel. 081 992 1612). A more convenient approach is via Acton Town Underground station (District and Piccadilly lines). Four giant Cornish beam engines are preserved at Kew Bridge Steam Museum, and may be seen under steam at weekends, along with a working forge and steam railway (tel. 081 568 4757). There is also an exhibition illustrating the history of London's water supply over 150 years, which is appropriate since the museum in Green Dragon Lane, close to the station, was part of the Metropolitan Water Board's Kew Bridge works which are passed (L) opposite a spur to South Acton on the North London Line.

Brentford, a historic Thamesside market town, was considered the county town until Middlesex ceased to exist as an administrative unit, although council business was conducted in London, meetings being held at Middlesex Guildhall opposite Westminster Abbey. A unique collection of automatic musical instruments awaits appreciative visitors at an unusual Musical Museum in the High Street (tel. 081 560 8108). Boston Manor (also accessible by Piccadilly Line) is a Jacobean house about half a mile to the north, standing in grounds which slope down to the Brent. Occupied as a private family residence until 1923, it is marred, like neighbouring Osterley, by the intrusive M4.

Crossing the Grand Union Canal beyond Brentford, observant travellers may soon catch sight of bridge abutments which carried the former Great Western Railway overhead on its way to Brentford Dock, where the company owned extensive warehousing. This short branch from Southall now terminates north of our route to serve an aggregates terminal and refuse transfer station on the Great West Road. **Syon Lane** station is conveniently placed to serve adjacent factories along the A4. Alight here and turn right for Syon Park, just over a quarter of a mile away. Syon House, an elegant mansion incorporating work by Inigo Jones and Robert Adam, occupies the site of a convent which was suppressed following Henry VIII's break with Rome. The grounds, reaching to the riverside, were laid out by famous landscape gardener 'Capability' Brown, who acquired his nickname because he was wont to tell prospective clients that their estates had 'capability'. Syon Park is a superb setting for one of the country's largest garden centres, a motor museum, and a colourful collection of butterflies which can be seen in simulated natural habitats. About a mile in the opposite direction (but perhaps better reached by Piccadilly Line trains), Osterley Park, whose noble estate has been slowly eroded, is the landscaped setting for a magnificent mansion which was remodelled in the eighteenth century, with painstaking attention to detail, by Robert Adam. The immense portico is based on a similar feature which Adam had seen at the now vanished Witham House in Somerset.

Wood Lane level-crossing heralds the approach of **Isleworth**, a riverside settlement whose fortunes were once largely dependent upon Syon House and the convent which preceded it. The Thames has often drawn artists to its banks about a mile away, a walk which may be avoided by boarding a Peckham-bound no. 37 bus. There is a commanding view of the river from the London Apprentice, a well-known inn of fifteenth-century origin which may once have been patronised by city apprentices. Continuing the journey through the western suburbs, **Hounslow** was formerly an important town far removed from London. Hounslow Heath, seen (R) after the train negotiates a triangular junction with the direct line via Richmond, struck dread into the hearts of travellers when in earlier days it was a haunt of footpads and highwaymen. It is long since tamed and reduced to a mere fraction of its original extent, pollution from vehicle exhausts now representing a far greater threat than vagabonds. Underground trains arrived in 1883, penetrating a kind of railway no-man's-land between the LSWR and GWR. Piccadilly Line trains still provide closer access to the main High Street shopping area, from stations at Hounslow Central and Hounslow East.

The direct route to Staines from **Barnes** passes **Mortlake**, renowned for tapestry production in the seventeenth century but now better known as the finish of the Oxford and Cambridge boat race. **North Sheen** preserves in the second part of its name a former name of **Richmond** (page 28). District and North London Line trains run parallel for a short distance (R) to terminate at their own platforms here, while our train continues via **St Margarets** to **Twickenham**. Orleans and Marble Hill parks are within reach of either station, although St Margarets is somewhat closer. In Orleans Park is the baroque Octagon Room, a surviving fragment of Orleans House. An art gallery here hosts temporary exhibitions and holds the Ionides Collection of eighteenth- and nineteenth-century illustrations of local scenes (tel. 081 892 0221). Marble Hill House (English Heritage), an English Palladian villa in a delightful riverside setting, was built for George II's mistress, Henrietta Howard, about 1725 and houses a collection of early Georgian paintings and furniture (tel. 081 892 5115). Twickenham is best known as the home of English rubgy, a game ascribed to William Webb Ellis, a 16-year-old scholar at Rugby School in 1823, whose individual interpretation of the rules of football heralded the founding of an entirely new game. The Rugby Union stadium is about half a mile away via Whitton Road. The continuing journey towards Woking and Weybridge via Staines is described on page 19.

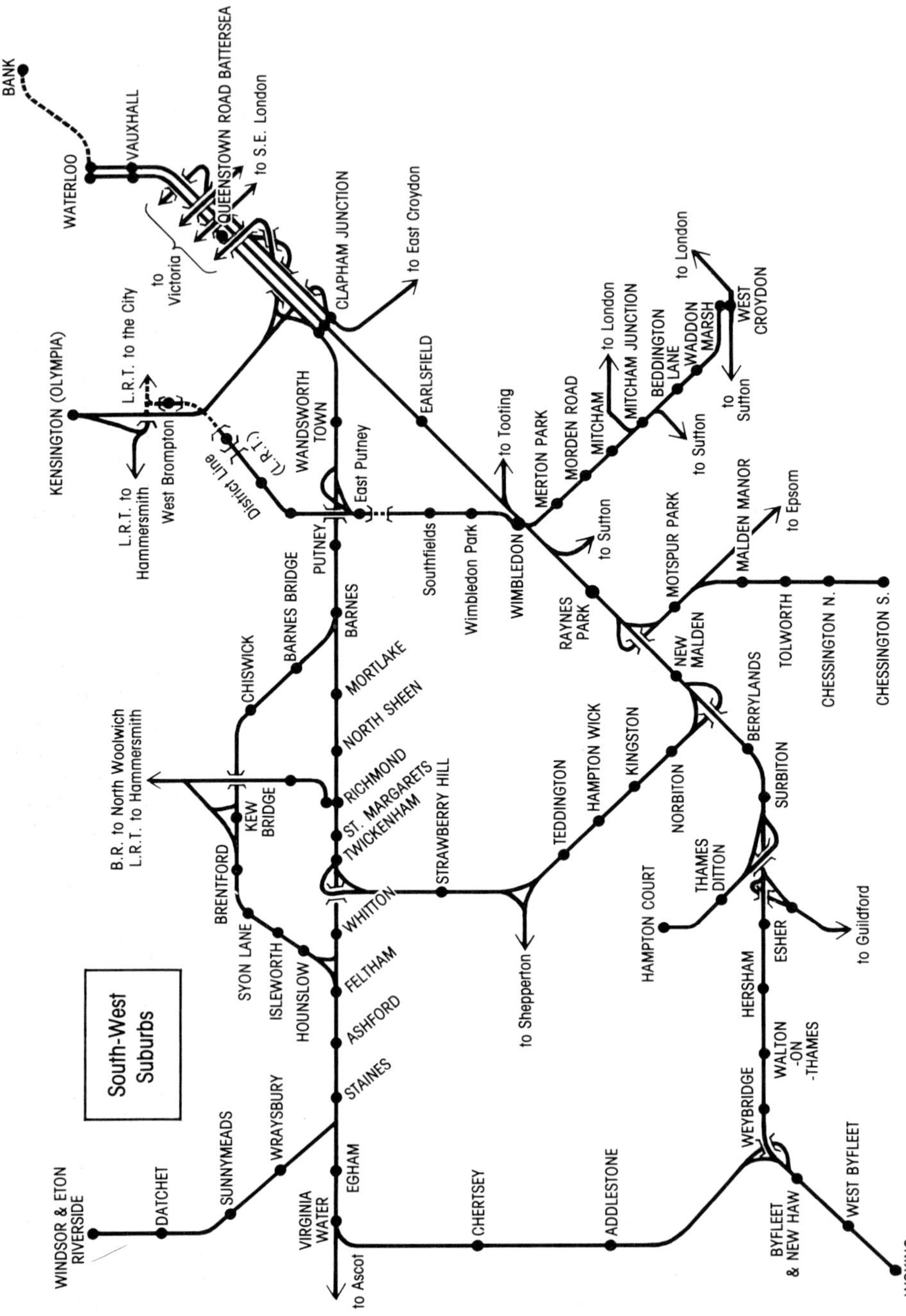
South-West
Suburbs
BANK
WATERLOO
VAUXHALL
QUEENSTOWN ROAD BATTERSEA
to S.E. London
to Victoria
CLAPHAM JUNCTION
to East Croydon
KENSINGTON (OLYMPIA)
L.R.T. to the City
L.R.T. to Hammersmith
West Brompton
District Line
(L.R.T.)
WANDSWORTH TOWN
East Putney
EARLSFIELD
to Tooting
MERTON PARK
MORDEN ROAD
MITCHAM
to London
MITCHAM JUNCTION
BEDDINGTON LANE
WADDON MARSH
to London
WEST CROYDON
to Sutton
to Sutton
PUTNEY
Southfields
Wimbledon Park
WIMBLEDON
to Sutton
RAYNES PARK
MOTSPUR PARK
MALDEN MANOR
to Epsom
BARNES BRIDGE
BARNES
CHISWICK
MORTLAKE
NORTH SHEEN
NEW MALDEN
TOLWORTH
CHESSINGTON N.
CHESSINGTON S.
B.R. to North Woolwich
L.R.T. to Hammersmith
KEW BRIDGE
RICHMOND
ST. MARGARETS
TWICKENHAM
STRAWBERRY HILL
TEDDINGTON
HAMPTON WICK
KINGSTON
NORBITON
BERRYLANDS
SURBITON
BRENTFORD
SYON LANE
ISLEWORTH
HOUNSLOW
WHITTON
FELTHAM
ASHFORD
STAINES
to Shepperton
HAMPTON COURT
THAMES DITTON
ESHER
to Guildford
HERSHAM
WALTON -ON -THAMES
WEYBRIDGE
WEST BYFLEET
BYFLEET & NEW HAW
WOKING
WINDSOR & ETON RIVERSIDE
DATCHET
SUNNYMEADS
WRAYSBURY
EGHAM
VIRGINIA WATER
to Ascot
CHERTSEY
ADDLESTONE

Meanwhile, Kingston line trains diverge (L) and a viaduct carrying 'up' trains clear of the main line descends among rooftops towards **Strawberry Hill** where Horace Walpole, eighteenth-century literary gossip and son of Prime Minister Robert Walpole, set about transforming a modest house into an exuberant Gothic Revival mansion, renowned in particular for a fantastic grotto. Beyond the station, the Shepperton branch makes a triangular junction (R), with Strawberry Hill depot occupying the intervening space. Stations at **Teddington** and **Hampton Wick** provide a chance to approach Hampton Court on foot across Bushey Park's wide deer-haunted acres (page 27). Teddington Lock marks the highest point to which tides flow on the Thames. In a few moments the train reaches **Kingston** (page 25), which spreads out before us as we cross the Thames.

On the route towards Woking and Weybridge via Staines, after the junction for Kingston, the train reaches the western outskirts of Twickenham at **Whitton**, where the River Crane passes Kneller Hall, formerly the home of artist Sir Godfrey Kneller but since 1856 home of the Royal Military School of Music. Unable to further its ambitions in Piccadilly Line territory, the Hounslow Loop rejoins our route (R) by a triangular junction at Hounslow Heath, contributing its trains for a combined assault upon **Feltham** where Lord Cottingham, Charles I's Chancellor, lived. An area of flooded gravel pits is encountered on the way to **Ashford** station, which to avoid confusion with its Kentish namesake is still styled Ashford (Middlesex), although since that county was expunged from the map the town has been in Surrey. Dominated by vast reservoirs frequented by aquatic birdlife, and uncomfortably close to Heathrow Airport, Stanwell is now virtually conterminous with Ashford, but can still show evidence of past centuries through the fabric of various buildings, notably St Mary's parish church and Lord Knyvett's Free School of 1624, which with its mullioned windows stands little changed by 300 years of history.

Staines is a Thamesside town which seems to be waging a losing battle for survival, pinned against the massive ramparts of huge reservoirs by suburbia's inexorable advance, overwhelmed by a surfeit of motor traffic and constantly bombarded by aircraft noise. Amid the tumult and confusion of today, it is difficult to believe that Roman legions once tramped where the A30 London Road now runs, and indeed no visible evidence of their station here remains. Boatyards add interest to the river scene, and just upstream of George Rennie's handsome Staines Bridge of 1832 a seventeenth-century monument, the London Stone, which may have given the town its modern name, marks the City of London's limit of jurisdiction over the Thames. Although Chertsey, further along our route, offers a better approach, Thorpe Park (page 20) may also be reached from Staines. On summer Sundays, buses 116, 216 and 290 operate direct. At other times, routes K10, 427, 436 and Green Line coaches 716/718 will set you down at Chertsey Lane, which is only a short walk away. Buses on most routes call at Staines bus station, off the High Street, but coach 716 stops at the railway station.

Forsaking the Windsor line (R) and crossing above the Thames, our train reaches **Egham**, the station for Runnymede, where a simple modern memorial reads 'To Commemorate Magna Carta symbol of freedom under law'. Here, after a long power struggle, King John negotiated a settlement with the barons which resulted in the signing on 15 June 1215 of Magna Carta. Offering little to ordinary people at that time, this historic charter, which sought to enshrine baronial privileges, nevertheless laid the foundations upon which individual liberty was built. A simple block of Portland stone nearby, in a three-acre plot which was presented to the United States of America, is a memorial to President John F. Kennedy, who was assassinated in 1963. Climb Coopers Hill for rewarding views and to visit the Air Forces Memorial, a silent tribute to Commonwealth airmen who gave their lives in the cause of freedom, but who have no known graves.

On the outskirts of Egham, Royal Holloway College, now part of London University, is housed in a flamboyant building based on the Château de Chambard in France. Dating from 1879–86, it was built as a ladies' college by Victorian businessman and philanthropist Thomas Holloway, and contains a small collection of art treasures.

Royal Holloway Sanatorium peers inquisitorially through the trees on pine-clad heathland at **Virginia Water**, where exclusive villas, each in the splendid isolation of its own demesne, tug desperately at the skirts of Windsor Great Park, and golf is played at Wentworth. The extensive artificial sheet of water which has lent its name to the district is rather more than a mile distant, along Christchurch Road, at the south end of Windsor Great Park. Virginia Water Lake and the surrounding parkland were created in 1746 for the Duke of Cumberland, victor at Culloden and later governor of the colony of Virginia. A lakeside colonnade, set up later, came from Leptis Magna, a ruined Roman city near Tripoli. Leaving the main route to Reading (R), our train encounters the M3 and M25 as it heads towards **Chertsey**. Chertsey Abbey was a wealthy and influential religious house, but following Henry VIII's differences with Rome it was suppressed. Despite suburban encroachment, Chertsey strives to preserve an independent identity, which if one ignores the proximity of the M3 is still evident by Chertsey Bridge. Thorpe Park (tel. 0932 562633), a popular and extensive theme park, is undoubtedly the major local attraction, and is reached by buses K10, 427, 436 or Green Line coaches 716/718 which stop near the station in Eastworth Road and Guildford Street.

Addlestone is on the fringe of suburbia and after crossing the Bourne and the Wey Navigation, trains branch off (L) for **Weybridge** (page 27), from where there are three services an hour (two on Sundays) to London (Waterloo). Julius Caesar according to tradition crossed the Thames hereabouts in 55 BC, and Henry VIII so liked the area that he had two residences: at Oatlands, which was destroyed by Cromwell, and Ashley Park, obliterated by developers. Visitors to Cobham Bus Museum should take buses K10 or 427 to Parvis Road, about three-quarters of a mile on foot from the site in Redhill Road. A special direct bus service operates on certain occasions (tel. 0932 64078 for further information). Trains for Woking take the west fork at Addlestone Junction, sweeping beneath the main lines from Waterloo, which are joined at **Byfleet & New Haw** station, alongside the former Brooklands race-track. A great deal of nostalgia attaches to Brooklands, the world's first banked motor-racing circuit, which during its heyday from 1907 to 1939 was the scene of national and international motor races, test runs and record attempts. After 1909 it also served as an aerodrome, but with the outbreak of war in 1939 the site was given over to aircraft production, subsequently passing to the British Aircraft Corporation, and is currently being developed as a business park. Ghosts may reputedly linger from the past, but a plaque recalling an illustrious history provides more tangible evidence.

Bridging the Wey Navigation once more, ribbon development extends through **West Byfleet** on the final stage of the journey. Approaching **Woking**, notice the Shah Jehan Mosque (L), founded last century by Dr Gottlieb Leitner, an Indian-born Hungarian and naturalised British subject. It was named for the ruler of Bhopal who largely financed its construction. West of the town, where urbanisation finally peters out amid coniferous Surrey heaths, Woking Prisons were opened in 1858; they later became Inkerman Barracks, after the last inmates were transferred in 1895 to Wormwood Scrubs. At nearby Brookwood a 500-acre cemetery is the largest in the United Kingdom, whilst Woking can claim to have the oldest crematorium, dating from 1879, in Britain. The restored Basingstoke Canal not far from the station is a peaceful contrast to brash modern Woking with its sparkling selection of shops, and soaring office blocks. Old Woking, away to the south, is the original village, but even here there is not a great deal of historic interest. For routes beyond Woking see *Surrey and Sussex by Rail*.

SOUTH-WEST LONDON II: WATERLOO TO OLYMPIA, CROYDON, CHESSINGTON, KINGSTON, HAMPTON COURT AND WOKING

by Ian McGill

This chapter follows the main line from Waterloo westwards as far as Woking, with the text arranged to also follow branches, in sequence, to Olympia, West Croydon, Chessington South, Kingston and Hampton Court. A multiplicity of frequent fast and local trains run every day, some, including those for Chessington, Kingston and Hampton Court, branching off along the way and therefore serving only part of the main line route. Normally it is necessary to change trains only for West Croydon (at Wimbledon), and for the limited services to Olympia (at Clapham Junction).

Setting out from **Waterloo** we follow for the first few miles a route featured more fully on page 15, as the train sweeps aloft on a broad viaduct which strides in a series of wide curves through **Vauxhall**, past the New Covent Garden Market (L), to merge with an intricate network of lines converging upon **Clapham Junction** from where in the morning and late afternoon (Mondays to Fridays) local trains leave for Kensington (Olympia), supplemented by two InterCity trains (Mondays to Saturdays) in each direction. Taking a mere eight or nine minutes for the journey, these services over west London's forgotten orbital railway offer an interesting and more pleasant alternative route to Olympia and west Kensington than busy Underground trains, and although potentially useful for exhibition patrons, especially those from south of the Thames, are not well publicised. Before continuing on the main journey (page 22), we shall venture briefly this way.

InterCity trains depart from platform 16 and crossing Falcon Road ease their way steadily downhill, ignored by the enormous illuminated advertising hoardings (L) which, greeting almost every other traveller who passes Clapham Junction, turn their backs to us. Negotiating a tortuous curve, the locomotive growls menacingly through a long, dark abyss beneath a vast expanse of busy tracks, where passengers pass constantly to and fro scarcely aware of this unsung byway. Local services normally leave from the low-numbered platforms, curving away from bustling electrified lines almost at once along a viaduct which sweeps in an arc to Latchmere Junction, where the two routes unite and pass the site of a former station at Battersea. A laborious climb to Chelsea Bridge ensues, and crossing the Thames at a sedate pace because of a severe speed restriction, we are treated to a panorama which is the exclusive prerogative of railway passengers, with Fulham Power Station upstream (L) and the new Chelsea Basin development close by (R) on the site of a former gas-works.

Trains now follow the course of the Kensington Canal, which except for its junction with the Thames at Chelsea Basin was filled in to accommodate the railway. Two bridges follow, under Kings Road and Fulham Road, but it is almost half a century since trains last called here at Chelsea & Fulham station. Stamford Bridge Stadium (L), inseparably associated with Chelsea Football Club and unique in English soccer history in having preceded the club whose home it became, now moodily ponders the future reflecting, perhaps, on how it almost became a Great Western Railway coal depot instead of the football ground which staged the 1920–22 Cup Finals, giving a new meaning to the Battle of Stamford Bridge. The District Line's Wimbledon branch hauls itself wearily away from a short subterranean excursion, squeezing briefly alongside (R) against the massive retaining wall of Brompton Cemetery. Passengers waiting at West Brompton station glance nonchalantly as our train clatters past beyond the platform fence, unaware that its grimy forebears once had the temerity actually to call alongside the District's smart electric trains.

Soaring to twenty-six storeys, the Empress State Building's bland triangular form (L) vies for attention with Earl's Court's huge concrete exhibition halls (R) which we pass unheeding, the sound of our train reverberating in hollow mockery from its blank, staring walls. Opened in 1937, Earl's Court claimed to be the world's largest reinforced concrete building and became the venue for many major events; some still take place here. Earl's Court District Line station was probably unique in issuing what was virtually a return platform ticket, enabling pedestrians to take a short cut between Earl's Court Road and Warwick Road.

Running alongside London Regional Transport's Lillie Bridge depot (L) there is a rare opportunity to catch sight of departmental rolling stock and locomotives used on the Underground. District Line trains emerge (L), confined to a masonry canyon, but a short branch creeps tentatively above ground, before venturing under busy Cromwell Road to reach Olympia in company with British Rail. Gaunt commercial premises (L) give way to streets of once elegant villas (R) as trains draw to a stand beside the huge exhibition hall at **Kensington (Olympia)**, close to the western end of Kensington High Street. District Line services to Earl's Court provide connections with the Underground network. A functional complex centred on the glass and iron Great Hall of 1886, Olympia stages many exhibitions and trade fairs throughout the year, and its limited InterCity services provide nationwide access to this important venue.

Formerly known as Kensington (Addison Road) after a neighbouring thoroughfare which perpetuates the memory of Joseph Addison (1672–1719), playwright and politician, this station is a mere shadow of its former self, when it boasted a multitude of train services and, incredibly, almost every track was electrified. Trains first reached here in 1844 when the West London Railway was opened from Willesden Junction, followed in 1863 by the West London Extension Railway from Clapham Junction. Severe damage inflicted during the 1939–45 war brought an end to most remaining passenger trains, including Metropolitan Line services, and London, Midland & Scottish Railway electric trains to Earl's Court.

Continuing the main journey, after Clapham Junction the Brighton main line swings away (L) across Wandsworth Common and the train enters Clapham Cutting, from which a now sail-less windmill (R) used to pump water. An embankment carries trains through **Earlsfield**, crossing the River Wandle, then a flyover carries 'up' local trains across the main lines, and an extensive depot (R) is served by a diminutive platform for staff use. District Line trains, having traversed a short Network SouthEast branch from Putney for the final stage of their journey, run alongside (R) to terminate at **Wimbledon**, where a line from Streatham trails in (L). Wimbledon Common and adjoining Putney Heath consist of over 1,000 acres of birch-clad heath and woodland which adjoin Richmond Park (page 28) at Robin Hood Gate. Baden-Powell wrote *Scouting for Boys* in the mill house of unique Wimbledon Common windmill, which is open most weekends (tel. 081 788 7655). Take bus 93 (bound for Putney) and alight at Windmill Road. Discreetly hidden in the grounds of a house in Calonne Road is a remarkable Buddhist temple, which may be visited on Sundays (tel. 081 946 1357).

The threat of further Underground incursions resulted in construction of a new line between Wimbledon and Sutton, opened by the Southern Railway in 1929–30, which besides serving areas of new housing also provided an additional, if somewhat circuitous, route to West Croydon. A quicker and more interesting alternative, however, is to join the two-coach train which currently leaves at about 30- to 45-minute intervals (weekdays only) from platforms 9/10 for West Croydon via Mitcham, taking care to board the correct train as these platforms also handle services for London Bridge, and West Croydon via Sutton. For those not wishing to travel towards West Croydon, the description of the main journey is resumed on page 24.

Our route to West Croydon is that of the Wimbledon & Croydon Railway, opened in 1855 and electrified in 1930. Slipping unobtrusively away past diminutive high-fenced gardens bedecked with flowers, the train encounters two busy level-crossings in the short distance to **Merton Park** station which is tucked away at the end of a residential cul-de-sac. The double track veered off (L) through separate platforms towards Tooting and although regular passenger trains ceased over fifty years ago, goods traffic lasted until 1975. Our train is relegated to a single line, whose spartan platform is isolated from the station facilities, which are located on the abandoned Tooting line platforms. There being neither subway nor footbridge, passengers needed to be agile as they had for many years to negotiate two derelict platforms and tracks to reach their trains.

Merton is steeped in history, although little obvious evidence remains. Merton Priory, founded in 1117, became a wealthy religious house where Thomas à Becket was educated. Destroyed after its suppression in 1538, fragmentary remains can be found along High Path, near South Wimbledon LRT station, and a Norman archway survives in the parish churchyard. Struggles between king and nobles continued even after the signing of Magna Carta, and the Statute of Merton in 1236 was a further attempt by the barons to consolidate their position. Merton parish church has work dating from the twelfth century and hatchments which include those of Lord Nelson, who was closely connected with this area.

At **Morden Road** a large industrial estate (L) was once the home of Lines Brothers' Tri-ang Works, whose products were familiar to generations of children. Water-meadows beyond are a reminder of what this area was like before it was overtaken by large-scale urbanisation some sixty years ago. Morden Hall Park (National Trust) stretches away (R) and although no longer frequented by browsing deer, it is enhanced by the meandering Wandle, whose water powered the wheels of a pair of snuff mills which survive alongside Morden Hall House (1770). Another mill wheel, which was part of the silk printing works of Messrs. Liberty of Regent Street, stands further downstream and may be seen from High Path.

Mitcham was famed for herbs, especially mint and lavender, and its past status as a prosperous village is still evident, particularly around the green, which was associated with the early history of cricket. Mitcham station, in London Road, is unusual in having been adapted for its present purpose from an existing house, the eighteenth-century residence of a City businessman, and from here to Waddon Marsh trains follow the course of the former Surrey Iron Railway (page 15). A short section of double track follows as far as **Mitcham Junction**, its platforms shared by trains to Victoria and Sutton, and which is situated on the edge of Mitcham Common, where in August the large Mitcham Fair is a popular attraction. Forging straight across the common the line, now single again, reaches **Beddington Lane** and another level-crossing.

Entering an industrial environment until recently dominated by huge cooling towers (R), the train pauses at **Waddon Marsh**, an island platform beside Purley Way, with footpath access to adjoining estates. Until Croydon Gasworks closed, this area was a veritable Dante's inferno, criss-crossed by a cat's-cradle of power lines where everything, irretrievably clothed in a mantle of black dust, lay beneath a perpetual canopy of steam and smoke, the atmosphere always permeated by noxious emissions from the gas plant; steel wheels squealed against steel rails, sending sound waves to echo and re-echo from soot-encrusted walls like the demonic screams of souls in torment. A tight curve brings our train round by Wandle Park (L) and alongside a line from Sutton (R) for the final mile to **West Croydon** station, built on the site of a former canal basin. Croydon has many associations with transport, for long before the advent of the Croydon Canal a Roman road passed this way, followed later by the coach road to Brighton. Railways found the town an irresistible lure, and later Croydon airport played an important part in the Battle of Britain and came to occupy an honourable place in the history of civil aviation before being usurped by Heathrow.

Modern Croydon is a major commercial and leisure centre whose success has undoubtedly been assisted by excellent public transport facilities. A bus station and LRT enquiry office is situated adjacent to West Croydon station, and an impressive array of shops is merely seconds away in North End, to which vehicular access is now thankfully restricted, whilst the Whitgift Centre is a traffic-free shopping precinct. Colourful Surrey Street Market has been popular for over six centuries, but the beautifully landscaped Queen's Gardens, a peaceful oasis watched over with paternal pride by the Old Town Hall (which now houses a library and information office), were completed only in 1983. Fairfield Halls, incorporating a theatre, art gallery and versatile concert hall, stage a wide range of entertainments. One of the few remaining buildings of historic interest is the Whitgift Hospital of the Holy Trinity, where North End meets George Street. These Elizabethan almshouses ranged about a quadrangle have survived unscathed since their founding by Archbishop Whitgift almost 400 years ago, when the Archbishops of Canterbury had a summer residence here. This was superseded by Addington Palace in 1772, which survived, albeit much changed, to become the Royal School of Church Music. Extensive tracts of wooded country such as Selsdon Wood (National Trust) and Addington Hills, south-east of the town, provide a complete contrast to Croydon's bustling streets.

Briefly resuming the main journey from Wimbledon, the All England Lawn Tennis & Croquet Club's original ground was situated in Worple Road (R), before moving in 1922 to its present Church Road site, which also accommodates the Wimbledon Lawn Tennis Museum (tel. 081 946 6131) portraying the game's absorbing history. Buses 93 or 200 go to Wimbledon High Street (Church Road). During the tennis championships the museum is closed except to tournament spectators. Sutton-bound trains curve away (L) before **Raynes Park**, whose platforms are staggered to accommodate burrowing junctions where Chessington and Epsom line trains branch off (L). The description of the main journey continues on page 25.

On the Epsom line, **Motspur Park** serves sedate inter-war housing, attended by immaculate sports grounds, and here Chessington trains, which run at half-hourly intervals each day to and from Waterloo, part company with those travelling towards Epsom. Intended as an alternative route to Leatherhead, tapping traffic from newly developing areas along the way, trains began running to Chessington in 1938 and although some work was in fact carried out beyond the present terminus, post-war financial and planning constraints conspired to restrict further development and thus ensure that the line was never completed as intended. Concrete was used extensively for civil engineering works and the branch stations are characterised by their strikingly effective 'Chisarc' concrete canopies, first encountered at **Malden Manor**. Aggregate traffic and coal continue to be handled at **Tolworth**, where Tolworth Tower rises twenty-one storeys to a height of 250 feet. Late 1930s housing at Chessington Court and Copt Gilders estates is served by a station at **Chessington North**, but visitors to the 'World of Adventure' should continue to the terminus at **Chessington South**.

In 1939 an RAF barrage balloon station was opened nearby, its buildings a conspicuous landmark for years after; the Ordnance Survey, evacuated from Southampton, later occupied a site along Leatherhead Road. Turn left along Garrison Lane to find the tiny church of St Mary the Virgin, of thirteenth-century origin and rescued from decay late last century. Most visitors, however, will be seeking the Chessington World of Adventure, a dramatic theme park which has been developed at the Surrey Zoological Gardens in the grounds of Burnt Stub, a fourteenth-century mansion which became a Royalist stronghold during the Civil War, was burnt out by Cromwellian forces and subsequently rebuilt. Suffering further fire damage in 1919 it was restored to house the administrative department of Chessington Zoo, founded in 1931. To the zoo and circus have been added spectacular rides and other attractions to provide hours of family fun and enjoyment, enhanced by the fact that rail travellers can take advantage of special reduced admission rates. If the prospect of walking proves too daunting, bus 71 will take you direct from the station.

Continuing the main journey from **Raynes Park**, a rash of modern battery hen housing (L) has extinguished for ever the brilliantly colourful pageant of flowers which once characterised Carters seed trial grounds. A broad swathe of grass (R) is the site of a trunk water-main supplying south London, and the distant wooded ridge of Wimbledon Common and Coombe Hill is visible beyond. **New Malden** was a decoy town during the Second World War, suffering heavy bombardment from enemy aircraft diverted from their intended purpose of attacking London. Clay spoil from construction of the Underground's Morden extension was dumped here during the 1920s, on land owned by a pottery which found that it made excellent bricks! Another burrowing junction takes Kingston trains clear of the main line, of which the description is resumed below. Kingston trains call *en route* at **Norbiton**, a mere half mile from Richmond Park's Kingston Gate. General Eisenhower used Telegraph Cottage in Warren Road, Coombe, during the planning stages for D-Day.

Kingston (officially Kingston-upon-Thames), by long tradition a royal borough, is the administrative centre for Surrey, although it has surrendered to Guildford the status of county town and become instead part of the London Borough of Richmond-upon-Thames. Kingston has a long history and the ancient Coronation Stone, preserved outside the Guildhall, witnessed the crowning of at least seven Anglo-Saxon kings. For centuries Kingston was the nearest crossing of the Thames above London, which contributed immeasurably to the town's prosperity. Refusal to allow trains into Kingston resulted in a serious loss of trade, but it was not until 1863 that the town eventually got its own railway station. A pleasing blend of old and modern, the excellent facilities of this major business and retail centre are complemented by one of the finest street markets in southern England.

On weekdays most trains (which run twice each hour to and from Waterloo) continue to Shepperton with connections at Kingston for Twickenham and Richmond (page 17). On Sundays there are two trains each hour which continue alternately to Shepperton, or to Waterloo via Richmond. However, the main line, which we left at New Malden, strides confidently past **Berrylands** and on to **Surbiton**. When the railway opened from Nine Elms to Woking Common in 1838, trains called at a wayside station just east of the present one. This was the closest approach then possible to Kingston, some 1½ miles away. Almost at once a new community, known in an early rush of enthusiasm as Kingston-on-Railway, began to develop around the station. This precocious child spurned its senior neighbour in 1855, and the upstart matured into a select suburb, one of the first dormitory towns attributable to rail travel. Thomas Hardy spent a year or so of his early married life here, and the writer Richard Jefferies, exiled from his native Wiltshire, lived here for a time. Later, Surbiton saw a pioneering innovation with the short-lived and now largely forgotten Surbiton to Okehampton car-carrying train, a forerunner of the Motorail network. Passing Long Ditton to enter Surrey, the main line – of which the description is resumed on page 27 – divests itself of both Guildford New Line (L) (see *Surrey and Sussex by Rail*) and Hampton Court trains (R). The latter ascend a tall slender viaduct to clear the main lines, then calling at **Thames Ditton** before reaching a Thamesside terminus. This short branch was opened in 1849 and electrified in 1916. Trains run daily at half-hourly intervals to and from Waterloo.

Off-duty members of the royal household at Hampton Court used to frequent Thames Ditton, which became a fashionable village. Historic Bridges Almshouses in

Hampton Court Palace

Station Road date from 1720, and were built by the owner of Ember Court Estate, better known today as Imber Court, a Metropolitan Police equestrian training centre. At St Nicholas' parish church a memorial marking the grave of Lady Edward Fitzgerald, whose remains were reinterred here after removal from Montmartre Cemetery in 1880, incorporates a fragment of the headstone from her tomb in Paris, which was shattered by a German shell during the Siege of Paris in 1870. This is a poignant reminder of a life tinged with sadness: Lady Fitzgerald's father was guillotined during the French Revolution, and her husband was executed by an English firing squad for complicity to smuggle arms to dissidents in Ireland.

Hampton Court was first opened to public view in 1838 and has ever since drawn visitors from far and wide eager to see the sumptuous blend of Tudor extravagance and seventeenth-century elegance which has been described as England's most beautiful and interesting royal palace. For current opening times and admission charges telephone 081 977 8441. A short walk across Hampton Court Bridge provides an opportunity for viewing the magnificent buildings to advantage in their lovely parkland setting at the waterside. Across the road, Bushey Park's broad green acres, frequented by wandering deer and interspersed with ornamental ponds, extend towards Teddington and Hampton Wick stations (page 19). The Cardinal Wolsey hostelry reminds us that this powerful figure of Church and State built the original Tudor mansion between 1515 and 1520 as his palatial home. Henry VIII transformed it into a royal residence when Wolsey fell from favour. Wolsey brought piped water from springs over three miles away, this supply continuing in use until 1876, and owners of land beneath which the conduit passed were until 1894 entitled to a supply of royal venison. A curious astronomical clock above the Anne Boleyn Gateway was made for

Henry VIII in 1540, and a tennis court of this period survives in the park. Charles I lived at Hampton Court, both as king and later as prisoner following his Civil War defeat by Oliver Cromwell, who when Lord Protector during the Commonwealth period also resided here.

Sir Christopher Wren was commissioned by joint monarchs William and Mary in 1689 to rebuild the palace and his work included a grand new approach, Chestnut Avenue, from Teddington across Bushey Park, with its splendid eye-catching focal point the Diana Fountain. His orangery was prompted by the recent introduction to England of orange trees, which were becoming a popular novelty in stately homes where they could be safely cultivated in heated conservatories. The last reigning monarch to live at Hampton Court was George III, since when much of the property has been devoted to 'grace and favour' apartments occupied by widows and dependants of distinguished Crown servants. The grounds of Hampton Court, featuring colourful gardens, immaculate lawns and cool lily ponds, were created by French landscape gardener Le Nôtre. The Great Vine, reputedly the world's oldest, was planted in 1769 and Hampton Court's maze, where Jerome K. Jerome's heroes of *Three Men in a Boat* succeeded in becoming hopelessly lost, is planted with hedges six feet tall and two feet thick. If after all this you have enough time and energy, and the weather is kind, continue across the park or alternatively stroll along the Thames towpath, to Kingston Bridge then via High Street to reach Hampton Wick station or turn right across the bridge for Kingston.

Continuing the main line journey after Surbiton, the train hurries west across Ditton Common, reaching **Esher** station which is virtually alongside Sandown Park Racecourse (L) on the slopes of Lammas Hill overlooking the River Mole. This is crossed before **Hersham** station, served only by local line trains. Esher's sixteenth-century parish church (not to be confused with a neighbouring Victorian edifice of 1887 by J. L. Pearson) has several features of interest, including a clock which uses cannon-balls for weights. After his fall from grace, Cardinal Wolsey retired to Esher Place, a fifteenth-century mansion by Bishop Wayneflete, of which only the brick gatehouse remains. Classical Claremont, built for Clive of India in 1772, and its gardens (National Trust) are also nearby (see *Surrey and Sussex by Rail*). Astrologer William Lilly (1602–1681) lived at Hersham.

Walton-on-Thames was the first in a series of five successive stations whose names began with the letter 'W', until this sequence was broken in 1961 when West Weybridge became Byfleet & New Haw. Walton is an interesting medley of old and new blending happily in their riverside setting, but the chief feature of interest is the ancient church. Oatlands Park, north of the railway, is the site of a palace built by Henry VIII, using material recovered from Chertsey Abbey, for his estranged wife Anne of Cleves.

Weybridge (page 20) with its interesting museum is an ancient town at the confluence of the Rivers Wey and Thames, where Charles I's death warrant is believed to have been signed at Ashley Park. A Tuscan column erected at Monument Green in 1822 carries an inscription in memory of Frederica, Duchess of York, who as wife of George III's second son lived at Oatlands. The monument was designed by an assistant to Sir Christopher Wren and stood at Seven Dials in London from 1694 until 1773. A line diverges beyond the station (R) to Virginia Water (page 20). There is a good view (L) of the former motor-racing circuit at Brooklands (page 20), alongside which a burrowing junction with the Chertsey line brings us to **Byfleet & New Haw** station. Ribbon development at **West Byfleet** persists to **Woking** (page 20), a busy and prosperous town which owes its existence to the railway, having developed on barren heathland around the original terminus of the London & Southampton Railway. Passengers for Heathrow Airport have an hourly Railair coach link which leaves from outside the platform 4 exit.

Richmond (*Photo:* John Armitage)

RICHMOND

by Olivia Bradley

Henry VII changed the name of Sheen (Sceon) to Richmond, to accord with his title Earl of Richmond, derived from the Yorkshire town of that name. Henry's Richmond Palace was later occupied by Wolsey, and Henry VIII's estranged wife Anne of Cleves lived there, but it was destroyed in the Civil War and all that remains is the gateway adjoining Richmond Green. It has some fine houses for company and nearby is Maids of Honour Row, built about 1720 for ladies of the Court. Long popular with royalty, the reigning monarch is still Lord of the Manor.

You could start your visit at the Old Town Hall in Whittaker Avenue, which has a tourist information centre, coffee shop and local history museum. Richmond's graceful bridge spanning the Thames was built in 1777, and although widened in 1937 still appears much as it did in Turner's painting. Steps nearby lead to the riverfront where you can embark on a boat trip or wander along to Terrace Gardens on the slopes of Richmond Hill; this famous viewpoint commands extensive prospects, and in the right conditions it is possible to see distant Windsor and the Surrey Hills. Return to the riverside path, passing Petersham village, with views of Marble Hill House across the water, to reach Ham House (National Trust), a fine Jacobean property.

The 'Lass of Richmond Hill' immortalised in song is said to have been Frances L'Anson who hailed from Yorkshire's Richmond, although the lady is also remembered in the name of a hostelry here. Just upstream, Eel Pie Island, which may have been named after a popular dish served at the island tavern last century, features in Dickens' novel *Nicholas Nickleby*. Richmond's chief shopping centre is based on the excellent facilities of George Street and The Quadrant, but there are also many smaller specialist shops worth browsing in elsewhere in the town.

Richmond Park is Britain's largest urban park and was enclosed from Shene Chase by Charles I in 1637 as a deer park. Large herds of these elegant creatures still roam freely among the majestic trees, lush plantations and rhododendron glades. The Isabella Plantation is an attractive water-garden, and Pen Ponds provide a haven for water fowl. White Lodge was built for George II as a hunting box and was the birthplace of the Duke of Windsor. Pembroke Lodge was originally a cottage which has since been altered and enlarged, and Thatched House Lodge is believed to have been built by Sir Robert Walpole, who entertained royalty here, and is named for the thatched summer house in its garden. You can leave the park by Robin Hood Gate and beyond Roehampton Vale cross Wimbledon Common, with its windmill. Join bus 93 at Parkside, and from a seat on the upper deck you will enjoy extensive views as it descends Wimbledon Hill towards the station.

RICHMOND TO NORTH WOOLWICH

by Stephen Sykes

The North London Link from Richmond to North Woolwich runs for twenty-two miles through the inner suburbs of west, north and east London and is a pleasant alternative to the Underground for some journeys; by changing trains at Gospel Oak, you can even travel all the way to Barking without going 'Underground'. Serving twenty-eight stations along the way, linking some of the most socially and culturally diverse areas of London, there are convenient interchanges with six other BR and LRT lines, the Docklands Light Railway, London City Airport and Woolwich Free Ferry.

The history of the North London Link is complex. Having opened between 1864 and 1869, and with links to many of the main lines out of London, parts of the route were used by several companies. Passenger services between Dalston and Stratford ceased in 1942 due to war damage, and those over the remainder of the route entered a long period of decline, culminating in a proposal embodied in the Beeching Report, but fortunately not implemented, which envisaged closure. By 1976 the basic service on the surviving western section (electrified in 1916 using the same system as the Underground) ran between Richmond and Broad Street, leaving the present route at Dalston and running south past abandoned stations at Haggerston and Shoreditch to reach the former North London Railway's Broad Street terminus, which also handled a few peak-hour services from Watford via Primrose Hill.

Meanwhile, diesel multiple units replaced steam trains between Stratford and North Woolwich and with support from the Greater London Council this service was projected westwards to Camden Road in 1979, thus connecting with existing electric trains and restoring passenger services from Stratford to Dalston, where between 1980 and 1985 four new GLC-funded stations were opened. In 1985 an extension of electrification (which had by then been changed to third rail) enabled these two basic services to be combined into the present through service. Thereafter Broad Street was served only by a few rush-hour Watford line trains which in 1986 were diverted to Liverpool Street over a new spur at Hackney, thus releasing Broad Street for redevelopment. These few trains, currently under threat of withdrawal, continue to provide Primrose Hill station with its only passenger service. A newly introduced fleet of trains runs daily every twenty minutes, with additional services at ten- or twenty-minute intervals between Richmond and Gunnersbury provided by District Line Underground trains.

Richmond (page 28), with good shops, a town green and riverside walks, is a popular destination with visitors. Extensively rebuilt in 1937, the station incorporates through platforms for Waterloo trains and bays, from an earlier station of 1869, used by District and North Woolwich services. These, after running alongside the Waterloo Line (R) for a short distance, curve away northwards past tree-lined suburban streets in North Sheen to reach **Kew Gardens**, station for the world-famous Royal Botanic Gardens, which are well signposted and about a quarter of a mile away. Essentially a place of scientific research which has trained many botanists and gardeners, many thousands of plant specimens have been assembled here, providing endless enjoyment for the many visitors. The collection dates back to 1759, when a garden was laid out around Kew House (since demolished). Later this was joined with the grounds of neighbouring Richmond Lodge to form the present gardens which were transferred to State care in 1841. A changing pageant of colour throughout the year, with magnificent floral displays and shaded walks by lake and river, the gardens also have some pleasant surprises in store, most famous of which is the oriental pagoda, built in 1761–2 by Sir William Chambers. Many of the more exotic and tender plant species are to be found in the humid jungle heat of glasshouses, the largest of which is the huge Palm House by Decimus Burton erected in 1844–8. An unusual garden laid out in seventeenth-century style adjoins Kew Palace, home of George III and smallest of the royal residences. Find time, too, if you have the energy, for a wander around nearby Kew Green (page 16) before rejoining the train.

Leaving Kew Gardens, trains pass the Public Records Office (R) and cross the Thames on a lattice girder bridge which has some unusual decorative features. Eighteenth-century houses line the riverbank at Strand-on-the-Green (R) and there are views downstream to Chiswick Bridge and upstream to Kew Bridge (R) with the pumping station (page 16) and blocks of flats beyond. Passing over the Hounslow Loop line (page 16) and under the Great West Road we come to **Gunnersbury** station, beyond which District Line trains veer away (R). Skirting the large Chiswick Works of LRT (L) and a worked-out ballast pit (R) which is an established nature reserve, a country enclave in suburbia, District and Piccadilly Line Underground trains rumble overhead. Bollo Lane level-crossing follows and a short goods line from Kew Bridge sweeps in (L) through a residential area at **South Acton**, where almost no trace remains of a short District Line branch (L), closed in 1959, from Acton Town, which was operated by one of a pair of unique double-ended cars. At Acton Gatehouse Junction (R) another short branch diverged to a terminus called Hammersmith & Chiswick; a further level-crossing is encountered at **Acton Central**, where the town hall clock tower is noticeable (L) as the train comes to a stand alongside Acton Park (R). About half a mile ahead, after passing beneath Western Avenue (the A40), the line runs on an embankment giving views (R) across to central London. Our immediate surroundings are now mainly industrial as trains pass over the main lines from Paddington, the Central Line, the Grand Union Canal and the lines from Euston before arriving at **Willesden Junction** high-level platforms. Low-level platforms are served by Euston to Watford, and Bakerloo Line trains (page 37).

For the next two miles the line, mainly in cutting, runs between the back gardens of suburban houses, serving stations at **Kensal Rise, Brondesbury Park** and **Brondesbury**. Curving eastwards through mainly residential areas, it then crosses above Kilburn High Road and under a viaduct carrying the Metropolitan and Jubilee lines to reach **West Hampstead**, a convenient interchange with two adjacent stations of the same name which are served by Underground and Thameslink trains. Almost at once another bridge is encountered, this time spanning the main line from St Pancras, and beyond **Finchley Road & Frognal** station a mile-long tunnel brings trains to **Hampstead Heath**, whose shaded lakes and leafy hollows shelter the stately grounds of Ken Wood, a Georgian mansion (English Heritage) housing the Iveagh Bequest Collection of important paintings and fine English furniture. For many, however, the wooded undulating heath is, as it should be, simply a place for relaxation and recreation. From its highest point (399 feet) near the Spaniards Inn (alleged to have been frequented by the highwayman Dick Turpin, who is still sometimes heard at dead of night!) London lies spread at your feet and it is possible to identify many famous landmarks.

Jack Straw's Castle recalls one of the leaders of the ill-fated Peasants' Revolt, while another well-known pub, immortalised in song, is the Old Bull and Bush, where builders of the Underground had second thoughts about providing a station after the platforms had been constructed, and so it was never opened. Among the sedate streets of Hampstead's respectable residences are Burgh House local history museum, a Regency property where the poet Keats lived and which contains Keats memorabilia, and seventeenth-century Fenton House. Also served by the Northern Line, you might find its station at Hampstead (incidentally the deepest on the Underground) more useful. Hampstead Garden Suburb, laid out in 1907, with a church by Sir Edwin Lutyens, is an example of twentieth-century suburban planning, but is better served by Golders Green Northern Line station.

Round by Parliament Hill Fields, sloping down to the lineside (L), we come to **Gospel Oak**, where a service of diesel trains connects for stations to Barking. In former times, many parishes observed the time-honoured custom of 'beating the bounds' each Ascension Day, during the course of which ritual a halt was made beneath an oak tree, where a Gospel reading would take place. In this instance the tree, which no longer exists, stood at the boundary of St Pancras and Hampstead parishes and its memory lives on not only in the name of the district but also in the name of a local pub, the Old Oak. During the next two miles a succession of embankments, bridges and viaducts carry North London trains at rooftop level, with extensive views on either hand as we sweep over a maze of tracks fanning out from St Pancras, to call at **Kentish Town West** station which, following its destruction by fire in an act of vandalism, faced permanent closure. With local financial assistance, however, it was eventually reopened in October 1981. Soon, a short line through

Kew Palace (*Photo:* H. Atkinson)

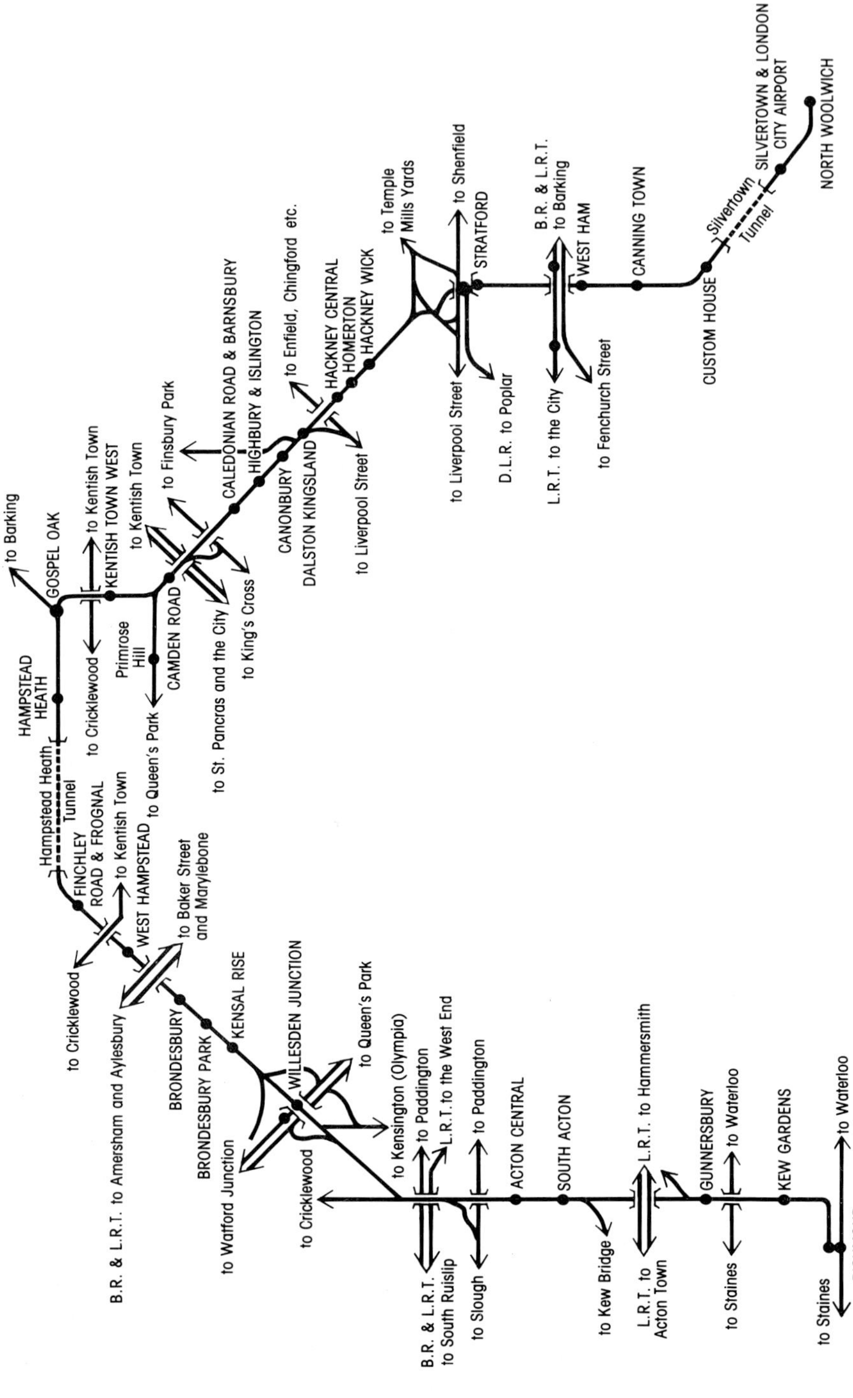
RICHMOND
to Staines
to Waterloo
KEW GARDENS
GUNNERSBURY
to Staines
to Waterloo
L.R.T. to Hammersmith
L.R.T. to
Acton Town
to Kew Bridge
SOUTH ACTON
ACTON CENTRAL
to Paddington
to Slough
L.R.T. to the West End
to Paddington
B.R. & L.R.T.
to South Ruislip
to Kensington (Olympia)
to Queen's Park
WILLESDEN JUNCTION
to Cricklewood
to Watford Junction
KENSAL RISE
BRONDESBURY PARK
BRONDESBURY
B.R. & L.R.T. to Amersham and Aylesbury
to Baker Street
and Marylebone
WEST HAMPSTEAD
to Kentish Town
to Cricklewood
FINCHLEY
ROAD & FROGNAL
Hampstead Heath
Tunnel
to Queen's Park
to Kentish Town
HAMPSTEAD
HEATH
to Cricklewood
GOSPEL OAK
to Barking
to Kentish Town
KENTISH TOWN WEST
Primrose
Hill
CAMDEN ROAD
to Kentish Town
to St. Pancras and the City
to King's Cross
to Finsbury Park
CALEDONIAN ROAD & BARNSBURY
HIGHBURY & ISLINGTON
CANONBURY
DALSTON KINGSLAND
to Liverpool Street
to Enfield, Chingford etc.
HACKNEY CENTRAL
HOMERTON
HACKNEY WICK
to Temple
Mills Yards
to Shenfield
STRATFORD
to Liverpool Street
D.L.R. to Poplar
B.R. & L.R.T.
to Barking
WEST HAM
L.R.T. to the City
to Fenchurch Street
CANNING TOWN
CUSTOM HOUSE
Silvertown
Tunnel
SILVERTOWN & LONDON
CITY AIRPORT
NORTH WOOLWICH

Primrose Hill, which provides a link to the Euston–Watford route, joins (L), its use confined to freight trains and peak-hour passenger services to Liverpool Street. Beyond is the Regent's Canal with the TV-am studios alongside (L).

Camden Road is about a quarter of a mile from Camden Town Underground station in a district developed about 1791 by Charles Pratt, 1st Earl of Camden and an eighteenth-century Lord Chancellor. A brief walk down College Street leads to the Regent's Canal towpath where half a mile away at Camden Lock a popular weekend craft market is held and, in summer, waterbuses depart for London Zoo and the colourful artists' colony at Little Venice.

The main line from St Pancras is crossed for a third time, then follows the site of Maiden Lane station (closed in 1917 as a wartime economy measure and never re-opened) and a bridge over the East Coast Main Line from King's Cross. There are commanding views towards both termini (R) across an area scheduled for redevelopment, and the West End and City skylines beyond are punctuated by familiar landmarks such as the British Telecom Tower and St Paul's Cathedral. Among the conglomeration of houses, flats and churches of bustling inner suburbs which crowd the lineside, a conspicuous white Italianate clock tower (L) standing alone in a small park and hemmed in by tall flats is all that survives of the old Caledonian Market. Entering **Caledonian Road & Barnsbury** station, the stock brick buildings of Pentonville Prison are visible (L) near the site of a nineteenth-century asylum for Scottish children. Caledonian Road Underground station is a quarter of a mile away along Roman Road.

Throughout its perambulations our route has become an intimate part of its environment, and this is especially so along the next few miles where leafy cuttings occasionally retreat to reveal sudden tableaux of domesticity or factory floor activity, and we pass almost close enough to pluck blooms from garden roses, climbing frantically to escape an overwhelming assault by bellbine, and nearly tangle with the billowing results of washday in small back yards. At **Highbury & Islington** there are connections with Great Northern Suburban (page 55) and Underground (Victoria Line) services. Soon a goods line emerging from a tunnel beneath Highbury Fields (L) trails in from Finsbury Park behind gardens long abandoned to nature where dusty sparrows lead secret unmolested lives at **Canonbury**. Abandoned Mildmay Park station, closed in 1934, precedes the site of Dalston Western Junction where trains used to branch off (R) for Broad Street through an area which suffered heavy air raid damage in both World Wars. **Dalston Kingsland**, the modern successor to a previous Kingsland station, was opened in 1983, partly funded by the Greater London Council. Former Dalston East Junction (R) is followed by the single-track Graham Road Curve, now little used and threatened with closure, but built to enable displaced Broad Street trains to reach Liverpool Street, the lines from which cross overhead almost at once.

The exit from **Hackney Central** station, opened in 1980, is by footpath alongside the original Hackney station building into Mare Street, a busy shopping thoroughfare, and about a quarter of a mile from Hackney Downs station, served by West Anglia Suburban trains (page 58).

Across the street on the left, public gardens have been created around a tower which is all that remains of the original parish church. Its eighteenth-century successor is at the far end of the park. Turning right, Mare Street leads to the Hackney Empire (still used as a theatre) and the Town Hall, and opposite are the public library and Central Hall, part of which is now the Hackney Museum of Local History.

Both church towers are clearly seen (L) as the train, bridging Mare Street, runs on an embankment to reveal views of the jumbled East End landscape. Hackney Hospital comes into sight (L) after **Homerton** station, which was restored to the railway map in 1985. As the train negotiates a bridge across a complex road junction at the end of the A102(M), a disused railway (R) leaves the site of vanished Victoria Park station. Part of the North London Railway route to West India and Millwall Docks, a section of it has been incorporated in the Docklands Light Railway (page 63). Victoria Park, alongside the old railway, was created in 1845; over a mile long, it was lavishly planted with trees and shrubs.

At **Hackney Wick** the train enters an industrial area dominated by railway yards and crossed by the Hackney Cut and River Lea. Goods lines branch off (L) to Temple Mills yard, and to serve a Freightliner depot and the huge London International Freight Terminal. As the train rounds the approaches to **Stratford** low-level station yet another goods spur swings away (R). Above, the bustling high-level platforms are busy with BR services from Liverpool Street, Central Line Underground and DLR trains (pages 63 and 100). An inner ring road effectively cuts the station off from the town centre, pedestrians leaving through a subway which leads to the bus station and modern covered shopping centre, where market stalls are set up on some weekdays.

The shopping centre leads to the Broadway, which used to be the junction of roads to London from Romford and from Cambridge, but is now the London-bound section of an enormous one-way system. At the former road junction is a memorial obelisk, with the parish church and churchyard behind. The east side of Broadway still has something of a town centre atmosphere with buildings such as the Victorian Old Town Hall, but the west side has been spoilt by inappropriate modern development. About half a mile along Romford Road is a group of late nineteenth-century public buildings, the municipal college (now part of East London Polytechnic), the public library, and the Passmore Edwards Museum, with displays on local history, natural history and archaeology. Maryland station (page 69) offers alternative access.

Leaving Stratford and heading south towards the docks, the busy High Street bridge carrying the A11 above indicates the site of Stratford Market station (closed 1957), which stood alongside a railway-sponsored fruit and vegetable market. Glancing back you can see the church spire and Town Hall tower at Stratford, and the tightly packed east London streets are lined with flats and houses (L) which stare resignedly upon a dreary vista of railway sidings, warehouses and industry (R) crowding alongside various creeks and channels of the River Lea. A green and white dome topped by a weathervane which crowns an ornate building about a quarter of a mile away (R) plays a persistent game of hide and seek. This is Abbey Mills Pumping Station, constructed during the 1860s as part of London's sewage disposal system. The line soon passes under a bridge carrying part of that system, the Northern Outfall Sewer, then beneath a railway bridge carrying BR's Fenchurch Street and LRT's District lines before arriving at **West Ham**'s low-level platforms which opened in 1979 to provide interchange facilities with the Underground.

There is plenty here to interest industrial archaeologists, with Abbey Mills Pumping Station only a short distance away. Although not open to the public, this flamboyant building which contains some exotic cast-iron work may be readily viewed from a cycleway which follows the Northern Outfall, and which may be joined about 200 yards from the station. About half a mile away at Bromley are some earlier industrial buildings, Three Mills, which harnessed the power of the tides to turn their wheels. These too are not normally open to public inspection but may be seen from an adjacent right-of-way. This is a fascinating area of muddy creeks, wasteland, derelict buildings, gasholders and industrial premises, but do exercise care, for paths shown on some maps are not always readily identifiable and it is easy to get lost.

A short run from West Ham brings our train to **Canning Town**, embracing an area previously referred to as Plaistow New Town or Hallsville, where the line enters the former Royal Docks which are currently being redeveloped by the London Docklands Development Corporation. Work commenced here more recently than elsewhere in Dockland, and as yet few new buildings (apart from London City Airport) can be seen.

However, things are likely to change very quickly and the old character of this district will soon be lost; at present it is a strange mixture of thriving industry and modern housing estates cheek-by-jowl with derelict warehouses and boarded-up shops and pubs.

Beyond East India Dock Road bridge are the lower reaches of the Lea (R), known as Bow Creek, and the gates of its flood barrier can be seen close by. From here a planned extension of the Docklands Light Railway will run alongside for about two miles before continuing independently to reach Beckton. As the train lurches east under Silvertown Way, built in the early thirties to relieve unemployment, there is little trace of Victoria Dock (Tidal Basin) station, which closed in 1943.

Many of the dockside warehouses (R), mills and cranes still stand, and the LDDC intends to retain some of these in its new development, but clearance is already under way, with new roads being laid out between railway and dock. The footbridge at **Custom House** station still has an extension, to which there is no public access, leading to the dock. North from the station a conspicuous eight-storey building faced with red brick is the Seamen's Institute, whilst the Custom House pub nearby dates from 1789 and provided accommodation for revenue officers, hence its name. Exhibits for a planned Museum of Docklands are currently stored at 'W' Warehouse, but may be inspected only during organised tours which are arranged by the Museum of London (tel. 071 600 3699). The train descends into a tunnel which was built in 1880 to take trains under a waterway linking the Royal Victoria Dock to the then newly opened Royal Albert Dock. Some fifty years after it was built it was discovered that ships were making contact with the subway roof and urgent remedial work had to be put in hand.

After the train surfaces, the former St Mark's Church stands forlornly amidst industrial surroundings (R), undergoing restoration for use as a Museum of Victorian Life, as we approach **Silvertown & London City Airport** station. Silvertown acquired its name from the premises of S. W. Silver & Co. who in the middle of the last century commenced manufacturing rubber goods here. So far little new development is evident, except for London City Airport which is about half a mile away via a signposted pedestrian route; the restaurant, which is open to non-passengers, provides a panoramic view of the runway, built on a stub of land between the Royal Albert and King George V Docks. Few original dockside buildings remain, but the docks themselves are used for watersports.

A walk of about half a mile along North Woolwich Road brings you to tiny Lyle Park, its riverside vantage-point commanding a splendid view of the Thames and its immense flood barrier, a marvel of modern technology (page 80). Leaving Silvertown on the final mile of its journey, our train is accompanied by densely packed housing (L), beyond which lies the City Airport. Tate & Lyle's huge sugar refinery (R) provides a curious contrast to the satellite dish aerials of British Telecom's Teleport. Arriving at **North Woolwich**, the station buildings of 1854, now a railway museum, are seen ahead, with preserved rolling stock alongside (L); a visit would provide a fitting conclusion to this journey. Exit from the station is through a new booking hall built in 1979 next to the old terminus. Until the closing years of the last century, this was a detached enclave of Kent, and from Royal Victoria Gardens which are on the site of a Victorian beer garden one can look across the river to Woolwich (page 80). Manor Way spans the dock entrances and is a good vantage point from which to observe redevelopment work, and a little further afield, sandwiched between road and river, is the derelict and isolated Gallions Hotel, built about a century ago to accommodate liner passengers who travelled here along a branch of the Port of London Authority's own extensive railway system. From North Woolwich it is possible to cross the Thames either by pedestrian tunnel or via the Free Ferry and return to London by train from Woolwich Arsenal or Woolwich Dockyard stations.

EUSTON TO ST ALBANS (AND CROXLEY GREEN) VIA WATFORD JUNCTION

by Stephen Sykes, Peter G. Scott and Hugh R. Fowler

Most rail travellers bound for St Albans tend to arrive by Thameslink trains (page 44), but Abbey station, terminus of a branch from Watford Junction, is more convenient for the cathedral and Roman archaeological sites. The journey from Euston does involve changing trains at Watford but with fast, frequent trains from Euston the entire journey can be completed in about forty minutes, and a good plan might be to make St Albans the focal point of a circular trip, using both routes from London.

The main line between Euston and Watford was opened in 1837 as part of Robert Stephenson's London & Birmingham Railway, which reached Rugby and Birmingham in 1838. By 1875 the line south of Watford had been increased to four tracks, but local services were limited. A 'new line', running alongside the main lines for most of the route, was built to provide a better suburban service. 'New line' services to Watford began in 1913, with Bakerloo Line Underground trains using the line between Queen's Park and Watford from 1917, and the London & North Western Railway providing through electric services between Euston and Watford from 1922. The main lines were electrified, with overhead wires rather than the conductor rail system used on the 'new line', in the 1960s.

Local services between Euston and Watford Junction are now marketed under the 'North London Lines' name. At the time of writing trains run at twenty-minute intervals on weekdays, and every thirty minutes on Sundays. There is also one, a service which may be withdrawn, in each direction (Mondays to Fridays) to and from Watford which does not serve Euston, but trains run instead via Primrose Hill and Camden Road stations to Liverpool Street. In addition, some Bakerloo Line services are extended beyond Queen's Park to Harrow & Wealdstone, effectively doubling the frequency over this section of route, but they no longer run between Harrow and Watford, having been withdrawn in 1982. The main lines are used by outer suburban services, some of which serve Watford Junction and Harrow & Wealdstone (in the rush hours a few also call at Bushey), and by InterCity trains, some calling at Watford Junction to pick up only (northbound) or set down (southbound). A branch line connects Watford Junction with St Albans (Abbey), its stations providing access to the eastern end of the Ver-Colne Valley walk, a fifteen-mile route linking Watford, St Albans and Redbourne. Electric trains operate at about forty-minute intervals on weekdays (hourly on Sundays), taking about fifteen minutes for the 6½-mile journey. There is also a branch from Watford to Croxley Green (page 40).

Euston was the first main line railway terminus in London. Designed by Philip Hardwick, its most impressive features were a 72-foot-high propylaeum (or Doric Arch) flanked by a pair of lodges, and the magnificent Great Hall, built in 1846. Despite many protests the Doric Arch, which had provoked criticism when it was erected in 1838, and the old station were demolished during the 1960s to be replaced by the present characterless and coldly functional buildings, fronted by a bleak paved area and surrounded by office blocks. Only a few traces of the old Euston remain: along Euston Road, on either side of the station approach road, are two small outer lodges dating from 1870, where engraved in the stonework are the names of seventy-two destinations in Britain and Ireland which could be reached, in some cases by very indirect routes, via the LNWR from Euston. A statue of Robert Stephenson which formerly stood between these lodges has been re-erected on the piazza which fronts the terminal building.

Leaving Euston, trains climb Camden Bank in a mile-long cutting, along which trains were hauled by cable until 1844, the engines being attached and detached at Camden. Glancing back, note the 620-foot-high British Telecom tower soaring above surrounding buildings. Emerging from Park Street Tunnel, trains cross the Regent's Canal (part of the Grand Union system, which eventually reaches Birmingham). Along the waterway (R) is 'Pirate Castle' a brick building housing a youngsters' boating club. Further on, the 160-foot-diameter Roundhouse (R) was built in 1847 as an engine shed, but ceased to be used as such in the 1860s and has since served various purposes, most recently as a theatre. Primrose Hill station can be glimpsed (R) on a short length of track linking the Watford and Richmond–North Woolwich lines. Primrose Hill, now a public open space, was once known as Greenbury Hill after three men who were convicted and executed for the murder hereabouts of one Sir Edmundsbury Godfrey. Entering Primrose Hill Tunnels, which are about 1200 yards long, the local line uses the 'new line' tunnels opened in 1922, whilst the main lines (L) use earlier bores whose southern portals are flanked by Italianate towers and side walls. Terraces of Victorian and Edwardian houses jostle for space with modern blocks of flats as the inner suburbs roll by, served by local line stations at South Hampstead, Kilburn High Road, Queen's Park and Kensal Green.

Near **South Hampstead** is the celebrated Swiss Cottage in Finchley Road, which has claimed to be London's largest pub. Rebuilt in 1965, the original structure, at first called The Swiss Tavern, dated from 1803–4 and resembled a Swiss chalet. Passing **Kilburn High Road**, look for the 254-foot spire of St Augustine's Church, visible (R) between flats and tenement blocks. A late nineteenth-century building designed by John Loughborough Pearson, this church houses a magnificent instrument by Victorian organ builder Henry Willis. The area once boasted its own spa at Kilburn Wells, and in Cambridge Avenue the animals' cenotaph is a memorial to all those horses, mules and dogs which died on active service in two world wars.

Bakerloo Line trains surface at **Queen's Park**, whose spacious four-platform station is a convenient interchange point. An unusual feature is that Bakerloo trains have to pass through the Underground car sheds before joining BR tracks for their journey to Harrow. Queens Park Rangers Football Club, whose present home is near White City, once played locally at Harvist Road. After **Kensal Green** station the train negotiates the short Kensal Green Tunnel, and then Kensal Green and St Mary's Catholic cemeteries can be seen (L), vast cities of the dead each lavishly endowed with elaborate memorials. Opened in 1832, the former is the last resting place of several famous people, among them Isambard Kingdom Brunel and his parents, also the novelists Anthony Trollope, Wilkie Collins and William Thackeray. There is an entrance to the cemetery in Harrow Road a few hundred yards from Kensal Green station. Approaching Willesden the main and local lines part company, the latter veering away eastwards to serve stations at Willesden Junction, Harlesden and Stonebridge Park.

Willesden Junction station offers an interchange facility between Watford line trains using the low-level platforms and Richmond–North Woolwich services (page 29) at the high level. There is a locomotive depot here, and Willesden Freightliner Terminal (L). A goods line linking Cricklewood and Acton passes overhead near **Harlesden**, and the factories of Heinz and McVities can be seen (L) alongside the main line. Wembley Stadium's twin towers are discernible (R) above the rooftops, whilst extensive railway yards persist (L) as far as **Stonebridge Park**, where the Brent Viaduct carries trains high above the North Circular Road and River Brent. Beyond the Bakerloo Line Underground depot (R) both main and local lines are reunited, and continue alongside each other as far as Bushey.

Wembley Central station is convenient for the shopping centre in Wembley High Road, but is almost a mile away from the stadium complex (page 85). Crowded inner suburbs have given way to a more spacious environment, where detached and semi-

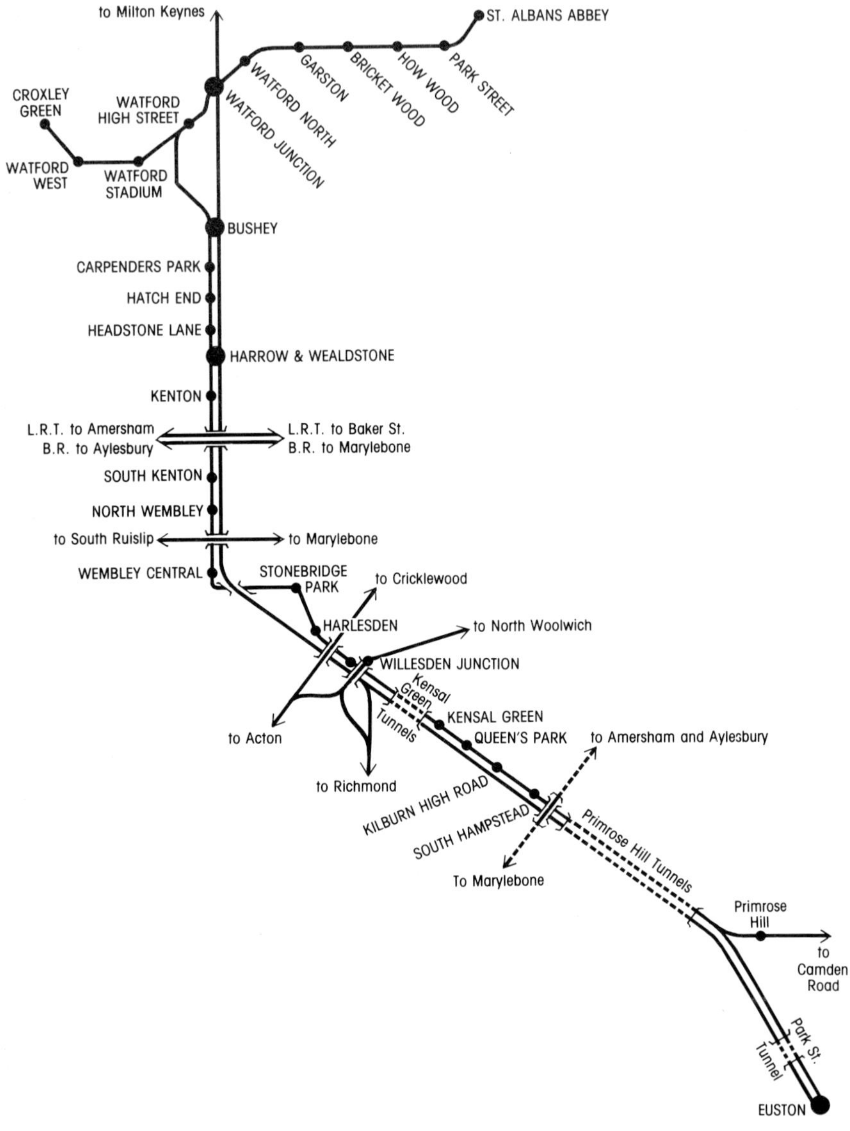

detached houses set in comfortable gardens are interspersed with pockets of parkland and small industrial estates. Much of this development dates from the 1920s, having been encouraged by electrification of the line to Watford. Marylebone–High Wycombe trains (page 83) pass overhead near **North Wembley**, where factories include those of GEC and British Oxygen (R). A fine view of Harrow-on-the-Hill unfolds (L) beyond **South Kenton**, with the spire of St Mary's Church soaring aloft from a wooded ridge. Nearer at hand, playing fields and the buildings of Northwick Park Hospital come into view and passing beneath the Metropolitan and Marylebone lines **Kenton** station is reached. Being little more than a quarter of a mile from

Northwick Park Metropolitan Line station (page 93) it offers a reasonably convenient interchange.

Around 1910, when the 'new line' was being built, architect Gerald Horsley was engaged to design its stations. Many of these survive in good condition and that at **Harrow & Wealdstone**, with its clock tower, is a fine example. Harrow Civic Centre is a good place to start a visit, since it has an excellent tourist information centre. Harrow-on-the-Hill, with its church and school, is the borough's main area of interest (page 98), and can be reached by bus. Harrow-on-the-Hill station (page 93) is, however, nearer, at the foot of the hill in the main shopping area. Continuing northwards, note Harrow's new Crown Courts (L) and the large Kodak factory.

A ten-minute walk south from **Headstone Lane** station is Headstone Manor, the earliest standing timber-framed house yet discovered in Middlesex. The house was begun in 1344 for the Archbishop of Canterbury. Nearby Pinner Park was first mentioned in 1273–4. It was then wooded and enclosed by a bank and double ditch, and was probably used by the archbishops for hunting. The railway cut through a corner of the park between the present Headstone Lane and Hatch End stations. The moated manor house at Headstone, its adjacent sixteenth-century tithe barn, and a granary (to be moved from Pinner Park Farm) will form the Harrow Museum and Heritage Centre. The barn and house are already open Wednesday to Sunday afternoons (tel. 081 861 2626; the manor house is presently closed in the winter). The tithe barn has an excellent local history bookshop, including books on local railways.

Pinner Hill (L) and Harrow Weald Common (R) lend the journey a more rural aspect, enhanced by wooded cuttings which effectively screen nearby housing development. Nearing **Hatch End**, a large Victorian red-brick building of 1883 (R), originally the Commercial Travellers' School, now houses Harrow Arts Centre. Hatch End station is a delightful structure of red brick and white stone, topped by a cupola and weathervane. A circular walk of some three miles, mostly by field paths, takes one to Harrow Weald Common where, having contemplated the panoramic view south to Harrow and far beyond, a country pub is conveniently on hand for refreshment. Nearby are the remains of Grim's Dyke, an earthwork of uncertain origin; a house named after it, and once the home of W. S. Gilbert, who died attempting to rescue a young lady from the waters of its ornamental lake, is now a hotel set in immaculate gardens.

Passing into Hertfordshire, **Carpenders Park** station was rebuilt in 1959 to serve large post-war housing estates. The estate to the west of the line was built in the grounds of Oxhey Place, burnt down in 1955. The seventeenth-century Oxhey Chapel, whose pitched roof and green and white bell tower may be glimpsed (L) beyond the station, lies about half a mile away, having survived both fire and developers. Soon the line is bordered by woodland (R), then at **Bushey** the local line curves away to the west, at the start of a loop which will take it close to Watford town centre. The hub of Bushey, which still has the character of a village despite heavy main-road traffic, is about a mile east of the station. The church is set back from the road behind a small green and duck pond, and there are antique shops and a tearoom. There are also a few buildings associated with the former School of Art founded by the painter Hubert von Herkomer in 1883, which made Bushey a popular place for artists to live and work.

Leaving Bushey, local trains cross the River Colne, flowing south to join the Thames at Staines. Swinging northwards there is a view (R) of the main-line viaduct striding across the Colne valley on a more direct route to Watford Junction. A single-track branch from Croxley Green (page 40) joins (L) before **Watford High Street** station, which is in Lower High Street near the beginning of the Ver-Colne Valley Walk (for which a useful leaflet is available from tourist information centres). Trains then round a curve to enter **Watford Junction** station alongside the main lines, passing a yellow-brick Victorian building (R) which was built as the London Orphan Asylum, but has been used recently as government offices. Local line trains terminate at bay platforms on the west side of the station, while the main lines are served by through platforms. Watford Junction station was recently completely rebuilt as part of an office development in a joint project with a property developer. The original station was a few hundred yards to the north and its single-storey brick building still stands beyond the St Albans Road Bridge. We now follow the Croxley Green line; a description of the journey to St Albans resumes on page 41.

In 1862, the LNWR opened a branch from Watford to Rickmansworth, and in 1912 a further short branch from the Rickmansworth line was opened to Croxley Green. Both branches were electrified with conductor rails. Services to Croxley Green were restricted to weekday peak periods following the 1947 fuel crisis, and passenger trains ceased entirely on the Rickmansworth branch in 1952. During 1988, services to Croxley Green were greatly improved with trains every thirty minutes on weekdays, but after this brief resurgence have once again reverted to rush-hours only.

Branch trains part company with Euston-bound local services soon after **Watford High Street** station, and shortly the remains of an abandoned curve once used by through trains between London and Croxley Green are barely discernible (L). This short spur was the cause of some acrimony when, following its initial closure in 1963, a service was briefly reinstated after alleged irregularities involving statutory closure procedures, but it finally succumbed in 1966.

Vicarage Road stadium, home of Watford Football Club, can be glimpsed (R), and Cardiff Road Power Station looms closer at hand as the line begins to swing west. There are traces of the former Rickmansworth branch (L) before the train crosses the River Colne and continues through a mainly industrial area, with stations at Watford Stadium and Watford West. **Watford Stadium** station (open on match days only) was opened in December 1982 for supporters visiting the ground of Watford FC and was provided as a result of financial assistance from the Football Trust, Watford Football Club and the local authority. **Watford West** primarily serves the travel needs of those employed at local factories. After crossing the River Gade and the Grand Union Canal in quick succession, trains reach an unpretentious single-platform terminus at **Croxley Green**, perched high above Watford Road and serving a predominantly residential district. Across the main road an embankment carries the Metropolitan Line to Watford (page 95). The two lines are only a few hundred yards apart at this point, and it has been suggested that they should be linked. Watford LRT station is situated about a mile from the town centre, and construction of a connection would enable Metropolitan trains to run more conveniently to Watford High Street and Watford Junction instead, connecting with main-line trains.

The coming of the railway transformed Watford from a small market town to an industrial centre. In recent years, some of the old industries have declined, new shops and office blocks have been built and the old street pattern has been obliterated by new roads, underpasses and flyovers. Most of the surviving older buildings are in or near the High Street, which at its lower end up to High Street station is semi-industrial and somewhat run-down, although some areas have recently been redeveloped. Most of the former Benskin's brewery has been demolished, but a Georgian house used as the brewery offices remains and is now an excellent local history museum, which includes displays on printing and, appropriately, brewing, as well as housing an enviable art collection. Further up the hill is the main shopping area. Just off the High Street, grouped around the churchyard, are St Mary's Church, the Bedford almshouses and the Fuller Free School of 1704. Now largely pedestrianised, the High Street continues northwards under a flyover to end abruptly where the main east–west road cuts across it, thus isolating the Town Hall and library, which can be reached only from the High Street via a subway. Near the Town Hall is an entrance to extensive Cassiobury Park (page 95) beyond which lies open country. Cheslyn

Gardens in Nascot Wood Road comprise 3½ acres of woodland and formal gardens, a feature of which are spectacular displays of rhododendrons and azaleas.

Continuing the journey from **Watford Junction** to St Albans, the LNWR branch from Watford Junction, opened in 1858, was the first railway to serve St Albans and although it was originally intended to continue the line to Luton and Dunstable this was never done. From 1866 the LNWR station (now St Albans Abbey) was also served by a Great Northern Railway branch from Hatfield, which closed in 1951. When the Midland Railway main line through St Albans opened in 1868, a connection was built with the LNWR's St Albans branch but this was never used by passenger trains. The Watford–St Albans line was electrified with overhead wires in 1988.

Trains leave from a separate branch platform on the east side of Watford Junction station. Although the branch is linked to the main line from Euston, there are no plans at present to run through services. Sweeping away from the main line, between the station car park (L) and sidings (R), the route at first traverses an area of terraced housing, factories and warehouses. Beyond **Watford North** station the former Odhams printing works, a 1930s brick building with a clock tower, can be seen (L) just before the train passes under the A41 trunk road. Alight at Watford North and turn right along Bushey Mill Lane for about half a mile to reach the River Colne footpath. Sidings (L) give way to housing estates served by a station at **Garston**, opened in 1966 and from where there is footpath access to the River Colne. Watford's built-up area expires where the M1 motorway bridges the line, followed by shady Bricket Wood Common, an outstanding wildlife haven which may be reached from **Bricket Wood** station, where the M25 passing overhead scowls at attendant housing below. Drop Lane leads to the waterside footpath, passing Hanstead House, a Central Electricity Generating Board staff training centre, *en route.* Hertfordshire County Council has provided a picnic area at nearby Riverside Way where the rivers Ver and Colne unite, providing a summer habitat for dragonflies and damsel flies. Moor Mill, reputedly more than 500 years old, was powered by the Ver but has not produced flour for over seventy years and now awaits restoration. Persistent residential development (L) is counterbalanced by mainly open country (R). Beyond **How Wood** station (opened in 1988) remains of the long-abandoned spur to Napsbury on the Midland main line (page 48) may be discerned (R), disappearing across the site of Radlett Aerodrome.

Park Street (formerly Park Street & Frogmore) station is on the old A5 road at the north end of straggling Frogmore village. Evidence from the Bronze and Iron Ages suggests that man has lived here since prehistory and a Roman villa is known to have existed in the vicinity. Frogmore Hall was set in grounds embellished with ornamental waterways, a trout fishery and golf links, but these have been obliterated by sixty years of gravel extraction, leaving a less picturesque legacy which is being adapted for leisure pursuits. The Victorian Church of the Holy Trinity about half a mile south is an early example of the work of George Gilbert Scott. Park Street water-mill dates from 1846 but ceased work in 1920 and is undergoing restoration. At Bury Dell Lane, part of the village green was taken last century for watercress beds, whose site is a favourite haunt of some wetland bird species.

The train is now in the valley of the Ver, which can be seen (R) immediately beyond the station; this stretch of river is often frequented by kingfishers, and adjacent wet areas are rich in flora and fauna. A wooded cutting is a reminder that this area was once covered by ancient Epwood Forest, which was largely destroyed by fire in the eighteenth century. Rounding a sweeping curve on the approach to St Albans, traces of the abandoned route from Hatfield can be seen (R) and Sainsbury's new store (L) heralds journey's end. **St Albans Abbey** station has been reduced to one platform with a shelter and a few seats, but the overgrown remains of a bay once used by Hatfield trains can still be seen. It has recently emerged that the future of Abbey

The Cathedral and Abbey Church of St Alban (*Photo:* Nick Lewis)

station could be threatened by a scheme to drive a road across the site, a plan which would also jeopardise the Colne Valley Transit scheme for a link between Abbey and City stations.

St Albans is described below. The town centre is about half a mile north of Abbey station, and can be reached on foot by turning right out of the station approach and following the main road up Holywell Hill. There are buses to the centre from a stop opposite, and some provide a link to St Albans City station and a possible alternative return route. To reach the site of the Roman city of Verulamium, or for a more pleasant walk to the town centre, go into the park opposite Abbey station approach and follow the River Ver for a quarter of a mile to Abbey Mill Lane; then continue straight on for Verulamium, or turn right up the hill for the cathedral and town centre.

ST ALBANS

by Arthur Miles

Visitors to this pleasant Hertfordshire town, with its massive cathedral, may wonder why the station at which they arrive has been styled St Albans **City** or St Albans **Abbey**; the answer will emerge as you read on. St Albans stands astride the River Ver, near the site of the important Roman city of Verulamium which was excavated earlier this century. One of the largest cities of the Roman Empire, it was the only one in Britain accorded the status of municipium, which conferred upon its inhabitants the rights of Roman citizenship. Much of it now lies beneath parkland, an ideal place to stroll at leisure on fine summer days and perhaps take lunch at the lakeside. The Roman theatre and large sections of the walls of Verulamium are among the more important visible remains. The theatre is of particular interest as it is the only known example in Britain to have had a stage rather than the more common arrangement of an amphitheatre. An extensive collection of Roman artefacts can be seen at the Verulamium Museum in St Michael's Street whilst later periods, with particular emphasis on folk life and social history, are featured at the Museum of St Albans in Hatfield Road. If you enjoy music and remember the large cinema and dance hall organs, do not fail to visit 326 Camp Road where there is a glorious collection of mechanical musical instruments at the St Albans Organ Museum.

St Alban was a Roman soldier serving in the city, who was converted to Christianity and became the first known Christian martyr in Britain. A church was built on the site of his execution. Later rebuilt by the Normans using material salvaged from the old Roman city, it became the abbey church of a powerful Benedictine monastery which came under siege in 1381 during the Peasants' Revolt. Following the demise of the monastery in 1539 the massive abbey became the parish church, a role which it has fulfilled ever since. Roman masonry can still be seen in this huge building, the second largest church in Britain, which has the largest nave (300 feet long) in Europe. At Waxhouse Gate, tapers and candles were made and sold to pilgrims. Among the treasures within are some exceptional medieval paintings, the shrine of St Alban, and many fine monuments. In 1877 the abbey church became a cathedral and the town was granted city status by royal charter.

Kingsbury Mill in Fishpool Street is a working watermill dating from Elizabethan times and houses a shop, art gallery and collections of agricultural bygones, and part of the adjoining miller's house has become a restaurant. Further downstream near Cottonmill Lane the ivy-mantled ruins of Sopwell Nunnery overlook the Ver, below a city of ancient and delightfully irregular streets lined by time-mellowed buildings reflecting a medley of architectural styles and periods. On Wednesdays and Saturdays, Market Place and St Peters Street are lined with colourful market stalls.

Appropriately, for St Albans is headquarters of CAMRA (the Campaign for Real Ale), many attractive pubs, some of them former coaching inns, are hidden away in its streets. Ye Olde Fighting Cocks, reputedly a medieval pigeon house, became an inn following suppression of the monastery and is claimed to be the oldest inhabited licensed house in England. French Row was thus named because French prisoners were held there in 1216 during a conflict with the Dauphin.

A fifteenth-century tower at the junction of High Street and Chequer Street is not part of a church but is one of only two surviving curfew towers in England. In medieval times the law required that fires be extinguished at a fixed time each evening, for which purpose a bell was rung from some prominent place at the appointed hour. The Royal National Rose Society was founded in 1876 to promote a knowledge and love of roses and its showground at Chiswell Green Lane comprises twelve acres of gardens planted with about 30,000 roses of all types. It is a marvellous spectacle which everyone will enjoy.

Gorhambury House, north of the city, was the home of Francis Bacon (1561–1626), a man of many talents who besides being a writer and philospher also had a successful political career, as a result of which he was created Lord Verulam. One cold winter day in 1626 his scientific inclination led him to contemplate the possibility of refrigeration, thoughts which were given practical expression by stuffing a hen with snow. The result of the experiment with the bird is not known but Bacon caught a chill and died. Salisbury Hall at London Colney is home of the De Havilland Mosquito Museum. In order to reduce its weight to a minimum, this famous World War II bomber was given a timber airframe covered with silk. Besides the prototype Mosquito, other De Havilland aircraft are on view together with a collection of Rolls Royce aero engines (bus 84, St Albans to New Barnet station via London Colney and High Barnet).

ST ALBANS AND LUTON VIA LONDON (THAMESLINK)

by Stephen Sykes

The former Midland Railway between Bedford and St Pancras opened in 1868, having been built primarily to provide an independent route for that company's main-line trains to reach London. Previously the Midland had used the tracks of other companies, who naturally gave precedence to their own traffic at the expense of the Midland's trains. A link was built between this new main line, from just north of St Pancras, to the Metropolitan Railway at King's Cross, thus enabling Midland Railway trains to reach the City at Farringdon and Moorgate. At Farringdon the Metropolitan was already connected to the London, Chatham & Dover Railway's Metropolitan Extension, which ran south through Snow Hill Tunnel and crossed the Thames at Blackfriars. This line was used by several companies, including the Midland, to provide through services between north and south London, but these ceased in 1916 and its use was virtually confined to cross-London goods traffic. As a result of Beeching era reappraisals, this traffic eventually ceased and the track was removed.

Meanwhile, through passenger services to Moorgate (which originated from the lines north of King's Cross, as well as from the old Midland) settled into a terminal decline and it therefore came as no surprise when the remaining trains, by now confined to weekday rush-hours, came under threat during the retrenchment of the 1960s. Closure did not, however, come about and in 1983 the line from Bedford to St Pancras, together with the link to Farringdon and Moorgate, was electrified and regular suburban services to the City were reintroduced. These reverted to rush-hour only in 1988, when the line through Snow Hill Tunnel was reinstated and electrified to provide a new Thameslink service from the Bedford line to destinations south of the Thames, including Gatwick Airport, Sevenoaks and Brighton.

On weekdays there are generally six trains an hour in each direction serving Blackfriars, Farringdon and King's Cross Thameslink stations before joining the Midland main line about a mile north of St Pancras. Of these trains, two run fast to St Albans before calling at all stations to Bedford, two run fast to Mill Hill Broadway then call at all stations to Luton, and two provide an all-stations service to Luton. During Monday to Friday rush-hours additional Bedford line trains run to and from Moorgate. On Sundays two Thameslink trains each hour run through to Bedford. St Pancras main-line station is now used only by InterCity and a few suburban trains, including an hourly night service. Some InterCity trains also call at Luton and/or Bedford.

Thameslink trains approach London from the south either via **London Bridge** (page 77), or by way of **Elephant & Castle**, where the station stands sombre and brooding on a grim grey viaduct, enveloped at night by an uncanny silence. The district, and therefore the station, is named after a former public house whose sign, the large gilded figure of an elephant carrying a howdah (misinterpreted as a castle) on its back, has been preserved at the spacious modern shopping precinct. Bakerloo Line trains terminate at the adjacent Underground station from where it is only one stop to Lambeth North station for the Imperial War Museum in Lambeth Road. Northbound Thameslink trains, however, wend their way among rooftops and over the busy lines from Charing Cross, where services via London Bridge converge (R), before crossing the River Thames to arrive at **Blackfriars** station, where some peak-period trains terminate.

Blackfriars bridge and the first station on this site opened in 1886, but an earlier bridge alongside (L) and a previous Blackfriars station just south of the river, both now gone, had been opened in 1864. Originally a red-brick Italianate-style building,

One of London's hidden gems: St Pancras Old Church (*Photo:* H. Atkinson)

the station was severely damaged during the war and was rebuilt in 1978 as part of an office development. Stone quoins engraved with the names of destinations as diverse as Margate and St Petersburg – which could be reached from Blackfriars, in some cases of course by continental boat trains – used to flank the entrance and are now preserved inside the station, near the ticket barrier. Immediately beyond the platforms Queen Victoria Street is bridged close to the wedge-shaped form of a remarkable late nineteenth-century public house, the Blackfriar, which is worth pausing to see. Standing on the site of a Dominican Priory, it has ornate stonework and is lavishly embellished with coloured granite, mosaic and beaten copper. Within, the decoration shows black friars (known thus because of their garb) attending to their daily chores. At once, trains descend steeply and enter a tunnel on a recently built stretch of railway which takes them beneath instead of above Ludgate Circus to reach **St Paul's Thameslink**, a new and as yet unfinished station below the site of the former Holborn Viaduct terminus, which closed early this year. The viaduct, built in 1867–9, is 1400 feet long and 80 feet wide, but because it is surrounded by buildings only the central section spanning Farringdon Street, which occupies a hollow where the River Fleet used to flow, is actually visible.

A few yards away the Central Criminal Court occupies the site of notorious Newgate Prison at the corner of Old Bailey, a name by which the court has become familiarly known. Newgate Street itself goes on to merge with Cheapside near St Paul's Cathedral, one of London's most famous landmarks. Designed by Sir Christopher Wren and built between 1675 and 1710, it is constructed of Portland stone and replaced an earlier church destroyed by the Great Fire of London in 1666. The sheer size and magnificence of the interior is best appreciated from the acoustically sensitive Whispering Gallery, whilst the Stone Gallery and Golden Gallery both provide splendid vistas across the City. In nearby Cannon Street, the London Stone is said to be the milestone in Londinium from which distances were measured along the network of roads which radiated across Roman Britain.

Emerging from beneath Smithfield Market, lines from Moorgate merge (R) as we

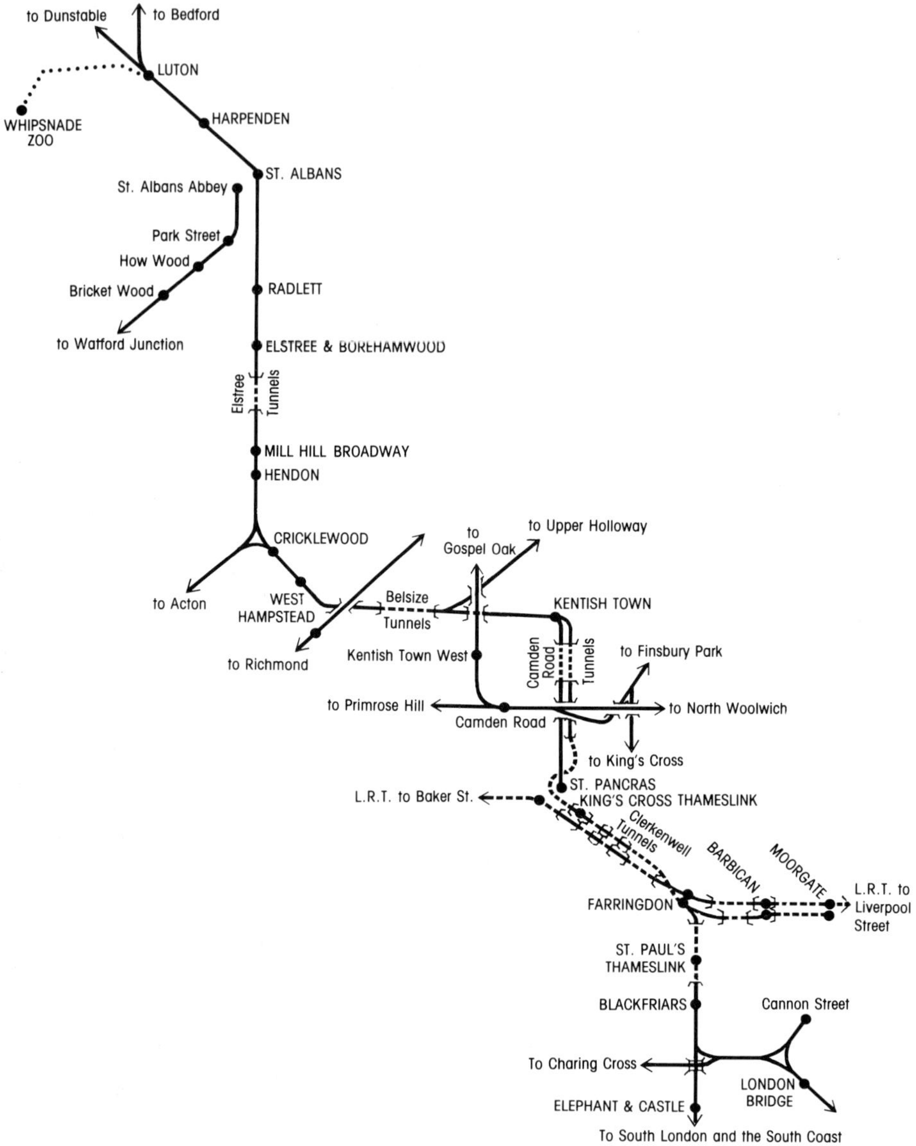

run into **Farringdon** station alongside Metropolitan and Circle Line trains. At this point the current-collection system for BR trains changes from the third-rail system to overhead wires and the pantograph of our dual-voltage Thameslink train is raised to make contact with these wires. This corner of London is known as Clerkenwell, where the Knights of St John of Jerusalem founded a priory on their return from the Crusades, and in the seventeenth-century the buildings of a Carthusian monastery became a boys' school known as Charterhouse (the Carthusian order originated at Chartreuse in France), which in 1872 moved to Godalming in Surrey. In the Middle

Ages miracle plays were performed here by London parish clerks, who lent their name to one of several fresh-water springs in the locality, which became known as Clerks' Well and can be inspected in the basement of 16 Farringdon Lane. Immigrant communities and radical thinkers played a part in shaping the later history of Clerkenwell, whose heritage is belatedly being promoted.

Slipping away from Farringdon the train passes beneath the Underground lines and through Clerkenwell Tunnels to reach **King's Cross Thameslink** station. Its entrance is in Pentonville Road some 300 yards from King's Cross and St Pancras main line stations, but there is a subway link with the LRT station. Already a major interchange, it is also the proposed site of a second Channel Tunnel terminal which would be used by international trains travelling beyond London.

St Pancras is one of the most impressive and least altered of London's main line termini, its train shed a single-span glazed roof 240 feet wide, built in 1868 by W. H. Barlow for the Midland Railway. The Gothic-style frontage facing Euston Road, opened as a hotel in 1873, was designed by George Gilbert Scott. St Pancras Old Church in Pancras road is an ancient building dating back to the eleventh century and although restored and extended in 1847–8 is well worth seeking out.

Entering King's Cross Tunnel, trains curve sharply beneath St Pancras, surfacing to join the main lines (L) as the North London Line passes above; they then forge on past the site of Camden Road station (closed 1916) and through Camden Road Tunnel to reach **Kentish Town**, which is also served by the Northern Line. About half a mile further on a freight-only spur from Upper Holloway joins (R) as the Richmond-North Woolwich route, in describing an arc through Hampstead, again passes overhead near a former station at Haverstock Hill (closed 1916), only to recross our path once more beyond the mile-long Belsize Tunnel under Hampstead Hill. Another forgotten station, Finchley Road (closed 1927) stood just beyond the tunnel. **West Hampstead Thameslink** is close enough to neighbouring Richmond–North Woolwich and Jubilee Line stations at West Hampstead to be regarded as an interchange. A predominantly residential environment follows, but at **Cricklewood** the surroundings take on an industrial aspect with an Express Dairy depot, warehousing and marshalling yards alongside. Goods lines diverge (L) to Acton before crossing the North Circular road and River Brent near the southern end of the M1, which is an unpleasant travelling companion (R) for the next five miles.

Brent Cross shopping centre, not conveniently served by BR, but tolerably close to Brent Cross LRT station, looms (R), and Brent Reservoir, also known as Welsh Harp after a nearby pub called The Old Welsh Harp, is adjacent (L). There used to be a station at Welsh Harp, but it closed in 1903 causing little hardship as it was close to **Hendon**. The main shopping area near Hendon Central LRT station and the old centre a mile away at Church End can be reached by bus (83 or 183), or you can walk via Station Road and The Burroughs, where an interesting group of early twentieth-century public buildings – town hall, library, fire station and technical college – are in marked contrast to the eighteenth-century Daniel Almshouses and Church Farm House, a seventeenth-century dwelling now a local history museum.

Sunny Hill Park looks out to Harrow Hill and the twin towers of Wembley Stadium, but from our train we see instead the spire of St Mary's, Hendon, crowning a ridge (R), and the site of Hendon Aerodrome (L), most of which has succumbed to building. Part, however, has been retained as an RAF Museum, illustrating the history of the youngest armed service, from early military aerial exploits over a century ago up to the present, and there are over forty aircraft on site. It is best reached by Underground to Colindale, however, as the nearest BR station is over a mile away at **Mill Hill Broadway**, where motorway construction has obliterated traces of a line which passed below on its way from Finchley to Edgware and which but for the last war would have become part of London's Underground. Suburban shops huddle round the station, but Mill Hill village about a mile away is strung out along a ridge with many interesting buildings; one clearly visible (R) from passing trains is St Joseph's Missionary College which has a tower topped by a gilt statue of the saint (bus 240).

Suburbia starts to recede now, and as the M1 sweeps away (L) overhead we dive headlong into Elstree Tunnel to emerge in Hertfordshire near **Elstree & Borehamwood** station where a building (R) still announces itself as The Gate Studios, a mute reminder of past glories. Elstree is a hilltop village grouped around a crossroads on the old Roman Watling Street west of the station, and may be reached either on foot or by bus (route 107). Marred by heavy traffic and not improved by recent building it is worth visiting for the splendid views, and a nucleus of older buildings, including some weatherboarded cottages around the church, remain attractive. Below the western slopes of Elstree Hill a country park has been created in the meadows surrounding Aldenham Reservoir, which was built by French prisoners-of-war between 1795 and 1797 to feed the Grand Union Canal. An abortive Northern Line extension would have terminated nearby at Bushey Heath, with a more convenient station for Elstree at the foot of the hill, but post-war green belt plans led to abandonment of the scheme, although some work had already been carried out.

Elstree itself has remained a village, but Borehamwood, originally a hamlet of Elstree, has grown into a town since the beginning of the century. The film industry arrived in the early 1900s, and London overspill housing estates in the 1950s. Although the film industry is sometimes described as having been based in Elstree, all but one of the studios were actually in Borehamwood. The main shopping street, Shenley Road, runs east from the railway station for about half a mile. All Saints Church (1910) is in this street; the two surviving film studios (one now the BBC Elstree Centre where the serial *EastEnders* is recorded, the other still used for film production) are nearby. By a roundabout at the end of the shopping area are the civic buildings, including the council offices, which provide a tourist information service.

A short stretch of open country follows the housing estates of Borehamwood, before a church spire soaring aloft announces the approach of **Radlett**, where suburban shopping parades and new housing estates have overwhelmed the original hamlet; but some attractive Victorian flint and brick cottages can be seen near the station. Following the line of Watling Street (L) for a while, the train passes a rail-connected aggregates depot (R) before veering away to cross the River Colne and the M25. Traces of an abandoned railway crossing Radlett Aerodrome (L) are remains of a long-defunct spur which connected with the St Albans Abbey branch (page 41). Napsbury Hospital was served by a station closed in 1959, and occupies an area (R) over towards London Colney. In a few moments the huge Cathedral and Abbey Church of St Alban comes into view on the slopes above the valley of the Ver, as the train crosses an abandoned line from Hatfield and approaches **St Albans City**. Do not be deterred by the uninviting prospect from the station, for St Albans has much of interest (see page 42) as you can readily find out by taking a bus, or following Victoria Street uphill to the centre and calling at the Town Hall tourist information centre. And there is an alternative route home, from the Abbey station (pages 36–42), for a change of scene.

Continuing our journey, little can be seen of St Albans, as the long cutting through which trains wend their way north does not open out until almost into open country. Rothamsted Agricultural Research Station (L) stands on the outskirts of **Harpenden**, a pleasant town with shops on the east side of its broad High Street set back behind grass and trees. There are also two greens just off the west side of the street: Church Green, overlooked by St Nicholas' Church (rebuilt in the nineteenth century but retaining a fifteenth-century tower), and Leyton Green. At the south end of the High Street is Harpenden Common, which extends southwards for 1½ miles. A branch (closed to passengers in 1947) diverged (L) to Hemel Hempstead, then between

Harpenden and Luton the line runs close to the River Lea, which flows eastwards to Hertford, before turning south to find the Thames. The river can be seen (R) before the railway crosses it on a viaduct at the village of East Hyde, the train hurrying past the site of Chiltern Green station (closed 1952).

The Luton Hoo Estate is spread out (L), with a lake just beyond the boundary wall and the house set on a hill. Approach lights for Luton Airport (R) are followed by the Vauxhall-Bedford factory, and the additional railway track which has appeared alongside (L) is a branch to Dunstable, the last remaining section of a former Great Northern Railway branch from Welwyn, of which observant travellers may have seen traces below the viaduct at East Hyde. Used only for freight in recent years, there are hopes of electrifying the Dunstable line and reintroducing a passenger service as part of the Thameslink network. Approaching **Luton** a view opens up (L) over the town centre, with the chequered flint and stone parish church close by.

LUTON

by Julian Sims

To many people Luton is merely a staging post, perhaps on the way to Whipsnade Zoo (page 50) but more likely somewhere further afield via Luton Airport, which is linked to the station by a frequent Railair coach link, the Luton Flyer. A purpose-built spectators' area means, though, that you don't have to come to Luton Airport merely to fly. The main pedestrian exit from Luton station is above street level, along a covered footbridge over the approach road and car park and the Dunstable branch line, then leading to a bus station and main shopping area, the largest covered shopping centre of any town in Britain.

Pub names like Boater, Panama and Blockers Arms recall traditional local crafts of straw-plaiting and hat-making which began in the seventeenth century but which have mostly been supplanted by other industries such as vehicle manufacture. Incidentally, although most of us probably know what a boater is, how many realise that Panama hats were actually made in Ecuador and merely exported through Panama? A blocker used forms of solid wood called blockheads to shape or 'block' hats.

St Mary's Church, already seen from the train, is one of the largest churches in England and dates from the thirteenth century. Well endowed with monuments, the interior also has other fine features worth seeing. There are also some notable Victorian churches, and an imposing Town Hall of 1934 has a clock tower rising to a height of 144 feet. Moat House at Biscot is the only ancient secular building, but parts of fifteenth-century Someries Castle can still be found, and Dray's Ditches and Waulud's Bank are evidence of prehistoric occupation. A Victorian house at Wardown Park, a mile north of the town centre, is now an art gallery and local history museum, and a museum of local crafts has been established in the former stable block at Stockwood Park. Information about the area is available from a tourist information centre in Alma Street behind the Town Hall.

Slightly further afield, Luton Hoo, a magnificent mansion in wooded country, was glimpsed earlier from the train. Designed by Robert Adam for the 3rd Earl of Bute, the house, now much altered, contains many treasures which have been assembled by the Wernher family, including the famed Wernher Collection of paintings by artists such as Rembrandt and Titian. There are also beautiful tapestries, ornate furniture, delicate porcelain and vases, as well as the fabulous Russian Collection of jewelled objects by Carl Fabergé. Outside, delightful formal gardens in a parkland setting landscaped by 'Capability' Brown never fail to impress.

WHIPSNADE ZOO

by Ian McGill

More correctly known as Whipsnade Animal Park, this is the country estate of the Royal Zoological Society whose headquarters is the London Zoo in Regent's Park. From a hilltop site high on Dunstable Downs in Bedfordshire, overlooking the village of Dagnall, this 500-acre park commands extensive views north and west across miles of surrounding countryside. Here on what was once derelict farmland many animals can, as far as practicable, roam freely in huge paddocks, representing as nearly as possible a natural environment. This was a completely revolutionary concept in 1931 when Whipsnade first opened to the public, as unlike a traditional zoo as the safari parks it later inspired. Thousands of visitors descended upon Whipsnade for the opening weekend, causing traffic jams for miles around, and the booking office at St Pancras had to stop issuing tickets to Luton. Even the local wild animal population arrived, looking for food, and the fence had to be rebuilt not to keep the captive animals in but to keep the native species out!

Since then Whipsnade has established a reputation for conservation and its breeding successes. Today there are over 2,000 animals, some – like Przewalski's wild horses and Peré David's deer (discovered as recently as 1825) – either on the verge of extermination or extinct in the wild. Others are more familiar, but like the tiger nevertheless often endangered in their natural habitat, so that the role of collections such as Whipsnade is becoming increasingly one of maintaining species which are no longer viable in the wild. Among the many birds, some of which are also sadly at risk in their natural environment, are geese, swans, ostriches, emus, elegant flamingos, and penguins, clowns of the bird world. During the summer you can also see birds of prey, such as falcons and hawks, in action, a truly remarkable spectacle. Many smaller creatures, domestic and farm animals, which youngsters can meet face to face, are resident at the children's zoo and in summer smaller members of the family can enjoy animal rides.

Some of the bigger paddocks are crossed by the Whipsnade & Umfolozi Railway, from which trains give a closer view of some larger beasts, including a famous herd of white rhino. If you prefer a picnic, several shelters have been thoughtfully provided, or you may prefer simply to laze on the springy downland turf and perhaps share your meal with an itinerant wallaby or one of the other species which wander freely. One resident you are unlikely to meet, however, is the huge white lion cut into the chalk on the western slope of the hillside, a familiar local landmark since 1935. You have to follow the road north through Dagnall to get a reasonable view of this beast, which is almost 500 feet long.

Whipsnade village, with its beautiful church dedicated to St Mary Magdalene, is worth finding time to visit.

Reaching Whipsnade involves a bus journey, but services run every day from Luton Bus Station. On weekdays there are some five suitable journeys in each direction at about 90- or 120-minute intervals, and on Sundays there are three trips each way. The journey takes about forty-five minutes and on weekdays the operator is Buffalo Travel (service 43, Luton to Hemel Hempstead via Dunstable and Whipsnade); Sunday journeys are operated by Luton Bus (service 245, Luton to Clements End). For current information telephone the Bedfordshire County Council enquiry line (0234 228337), Mondays to Fridays 8 a.m. to 6 p.m. At a car park opposite the main entrance an apparently over-generous provision of bus stops and shelters (mostly of London Transport vintage) date from the zoo's early days when most visitors came by public transport, instead of being individually packaged in little tin boxes or elephantine motor coaches.

GREAT NORTHERN SUBURBAN: KING'S CROSS/MOORGATE TO HERTFORD AND HITCHIN

by Stephen Sykes

The Great Northern Railway opened its line between Peterborough and London in 1850, as part of the route from Doncaster. At first passenger trains used a station at Maiden Lane, until the line was extended to the new King's Cross terminus in 1852. A branch from Alexandra Palace to Enfield was opened in 1871 and later extended to form a loop through Hertford, rejoining the main line near Stevenage, primarily to relieve congestion on the main line by providing an alternative route. The Hertford loop was opened to Cuffley in 1910; the remaining section opened for freight trains in 1918, but passenger services did not begin until 1924. At the London end of the route, several lines were constructed to enable suburban trains to serve the City; thus in 1863 the GN was linked at King's Cross to the Metropolitan Railway, trains running through to Farringdon (and, later, to Moorgate and to south London).

In 1875 a line was opened linking the GN near Finsbury Park to the North London Railway, which began running suburban services to its Broad Street terminus. In 1904, the Great Northern and City tube line opened between Finsbury Park and Moorgate, via Drayton Park. It had been intended to link this line to the Great Northern suburban routes, but in fact it operated as a separate service, terminating in underground platforms at Finsbury Park. Taken over by the Metropolitan Railway in 1913, it was later operated as a branch of the Underground's Northern Line. By the early 1970s services to the City had declined, and the Moorgate tube was cut back in 1964 to Drayton Park so that between here and Finsbury Park it could be incorporated in the new Victoria Line.

With the advent of suburban electrification new 'Great Northern Electric' services were introduced in 1976, and using connections from the old Northern Line at Drayton Park to the surface at Finsbury Park, these at last provided a through route to the Moorgate tube. Remaining services from GN stations to Farringdon and Broad Street were then withdrawn. Electrification was later extended, reaching Royston in 1978, Huntingdon in 1986, Peterborough in 1987 and Cambridge in 1988. InterCity electric services to Leeds began in 1989, and services to Edinburgh are due to begin in 1991.

Inner suburban services run via the main line to Welwyn Garden City, and via the loop line to Hertford North, with some journeys extended to Stevenage. These trains use Moorgate mostly (Mondays to Fridays), but in the very early morning and late evening, and at weekends, they are diverted to and from King's Cross instead. The basic weekday service calls at all stations, running every fifteen minutes to Alexandra Palace, with trains continuing alternately on the main line or the loop, giving both Welwyn Garden City and Hertford North a thirty-minute service. On Sundays there are hourly services to Welwyn Garden City and to Stevenage via Hertford North.

Outer suburban trains, which run from King's Cross, offer a half-hourly semi-fast service on weekdays to Welwyn Garden City, then call at all stations to Hitchin *en route* to Letchworth or Royston. There are two trains each hour to Cambridge, one calling only at Stevenage and the other calling at Finsbury Park, Stevenage and all stations. An hourly service to Peterborough calls at Finsbury Park, Stevenage, Hitchin and all stations, supplemented by hourly trains to Huntingdon via the Hertford Loop, which stop at Finsbury Park, Hertford North and all stations. On Sundays there are two outer suburban services each hour, via the main line, to Cambridge and Peterborough. The only intermediate station served by InterCity trains is Stevenage, which has services to Yorkshire, the north-east, and Scotland.

For centuries the district now invariably referred to as King's Cross was known as Battlebridge, being so called by Dickens in *Oliver Twist*, and still remembered in Battle Bridge Road. This supposedly commemorates a battle between Boadicea and the advancing Romans in AD 60, but the present name came about because of a statue of King George IV which for twelve years from 1833 until 1845 stood at the intersection of the present Euston, Pentonville and Gray's Inn roads. King's Cross station, opened in 1852, was designed by the architect Lewis Cubitt, whose uncle and cousin were engineers and also involved in the construction of the Great Northern Railway. The clock which adorns the station's prominent tower was originally at the Crystal Palace in Hyde Park during the Great Exhibition of 1851. Behind the yellow brick frontage are two train sheds, each 150 feet wide and 800 feet long. Also by Cubitt, the adjoining stock brick Great Northern Hotel was opened in 1854. A modern ticket office and concourse date from 1973. Some GN services use the main line platforms, but many depart from separate suburban platforms.

King's Cross–Hitchin
Leaving the terminus, St Pancras station can be seen (L) before the train immediately enters Gasworks Tunnel, emerging briefly to pass under a viaduct carrying the Richmond–North Woolwich line (page 29) and then plunging into Copenhagen Tunnel, named from its proximity to Copenhagen Tavern, site of a seventeenth-century residence of the Danish ambassador. Once the train is in the open again, the Highbury Stadium home of Arsenal Football Club, which moved across the river from Woolwich in 1913, can be glimpsed a quarter of a mile away across the rooftops (R) as we approach **Finsbury Park**, an interchange with Moorgate, LRT, and London Buses services. Heading north between the park itself (R) and Stroud Green (L), we pass over the Gospel Oak–Barking line near **Harringay** (about a quarter of a mile from Harringay East station), and alongside Network SouthEast's Hornsey depot, where a large sign gives the mileages to 'Edinburgh 389, London 4'.

Beyond **Hornsey**, an endless sea of rooftops disperse to reveal the elephantine form of Alexandra Palace (L), crowning the breezy Northern Heights which rise ahead as we approach Wood Green (now **Alexandra Palace**) station, close to the park entrance. Dogged by misfortune, some say the result of a gypsy curse, since its inception in 1873, 'Ally Pally' as it later became affectionately known had, literally, a baptism of fire when it was burnt out shortly after opening, but it was later rebuilt. In 1936 the BBC, which still has a transmitter here, began broadcasting Britain's first public television service from Alexandra Palace. A further disastrous fire occurred in 1980, but the complex has since been restored as a venue for conferences, shows and exhibitions; the 200 acres of parkland in which it is set has a boating lake, ski slope and other facilities, but the former racecourse closed in 1970.

InterCity trains are maintained at Bounds Green depot (L) and the Hertford Loop (page 55) branches off, a flyover carrying 'down' trains across the main lines which, except for short stretches at Welwyn Viaduct and Tunnels, continue as four tracks for the next fifty miles. The train thunders through Wood Green Tunnels and over the North Circular Road, Friern Hospital lying alongside (L) near **New Southgate**, which is followed by Barnet Tunnel and stations at **Oakleigh Park** and **New Barnet**, each surrounded by dormitory suburbs. Barnet, over a mile away (buses 84 and 107), is better served by High Barnet station (Northern Line). Once a noted spa, its much abused well house, rebuilt in 1922, still stands on an estate in Wells Road, and further away at Arkley (bus 107) there is a fine windmill.

As we enter rural surroundings, a cutting takes us near Monken Hadley, site of the Battle of Barnet fought in 1471 during the Wars of the Roses, then **Hadley Wood** station intervenes between two closely spaced tunnels. Also known as Monken Hadley Common, the surrounding country, a fragment of Enfield Chase (page 56),

The well house at Barnet (*Photo:* I. McGill)

stretches eastwards to Cockfosters (Piccadilly Line) station for Trent Country Park. The train emerges from yet another tunnel to reach **Potters Bar**, where one of the oldest buildings, Wyllots Manor, a timber-framed structure, is surrounded by railway-generated development near the station. The original town centre is about three-quarters of a mile east along the old Great North Road where some older buildings co-exist with more modern neighbours. Fields and woods form a buffer zone around **Brookmans Park**, overlooked by the distant masts of a radio transmitting station (R) about a mile away. **Welham Green** station opened in 1986 following a campaign by local residents. Hatfield Park lies beyond the old Great North Road (R) which accompanies the railway line for the next two miles to **Hatfield**.

Old Hatfield (R) is a few minutes' walk from the station, from where a private driveway built last century provided direct access to Hatfield House, whose chimneys and clock tower are visible beyond the church (R). Much redevelopment took place during the 1960s and 1970s, but there are vestiges of an older town near the parish church. Hatfield House dates from the early seventeenth century and was built for Robert Cecil, 1st Earl of Salisbury, on the site of a medieval Bishops' Palace. The house was partially destroyed by a spectacular fire in 1835, when one of the reporters present was Charles Dickens, then a journalist with the *Morning Chronicle*. Hatfield House and its magnificent gardens are open during the summer, and Elizabethan-style banquets are held throughout the year in a surviving wing of the old palace. There is heritage of a different kind in a local museum and working watermill at Mill Green, where milling can sometimes be seen in progress and stone-ground flour may be bought (tel. 07072 71362). Modern Hatfield really dates from the opening of De Havilland's aircraft factory some sixty years ago, and was designated a New Town in 1948.

Hurrying onward across a valley watered by the River Lea (or Lee), which flows through Hertford and Ware before turning south to join the Thames, the train heads for **Welwyn Garden City**. A new shopping centre (L) will provide future access to the station, whose handsome Georgian-style buildings of 1926, designed to harmonise with surrounding shops and town centre buildings, have been demolished. A tourist information centre at Campus West, half a mile away, shares accommodation with a library, theatre and café. A town trail leaflet available here describes a suggested tour of the city centre, illustrating development of the garden city concept as visualised by its pioneer, Sir Ebenezer Howard. If you wish to pursue the subject further, a newly created First Garden City Museum at Letchworth will also be of interest (first station beyond Hitchin when travelling towards Cambridge) but is outside the scope of this book. Starting on the western outskirts of the city, Ayot Greenway is a 2½-mile path, open to walkers, cyclists and horse riders, which has much wildlife interest and was converted from an old railway.

Note the Shredded Wheat factory (R), built in 1925, before the townscape disperses and we are borne aloft on the graceful Welwyn (or Digswell) viaduct high above the River Mimram. **Welwyn North** station is some distance from Welwyn, a former coaching town beyond the A1(M) which runs parallel about a mile away (L), striding above Welwyn Roman Baths which have been uniquely preserved in a steel vault beneath the carriageways. About thirty minutes' walk from the station, the baths' opening times are restricted and intending visitors are advised to enquire before setting out (tel: 07072 71362). Approaching **Knebworth**, note the bell tower of St Martin's Church (L), a building designed earlier this century by Sir Edwin Lutyens. An old vine has been preserved at the station, inside the 'down' platform shelter. The old village is about 1½ miles away, clustered about Knebworth House, a Tudor manor house which was transformed in exuberant Gothic style 150 years ago, one of its finest assets being the sumptuous State Drawing Room.

Heading north beside a golf course (L), the line is rejoined by the Hertford loop at Langley Junction and soon the outlying estates of **Stevenage** can be seen. In 1946 it was designated the first New Town, and a modern town centre, one of the earliest large-scale traffic-free centres in Europe, was built in 1958. The present station was opened in 1973, replacing the original premises in the old town further north, and is linked by footbridge to a modern leisure complex and theatre. Shops and public buildings nearby include a library with tourist information facilities, and in Cavendish Road ICL has assembled a collection and archives relating to computer history (open by appointment only, tel. 0438 31331, ext. 528). In contrast, the 150-acre Fairlands Valley Park has a large lake devoted to sailing and fishing, with facilities for other outdoor activities. Stevenage has a museum in the undercroft of modern St George's Church, but dedicated gardeners might prefer to visit Stevenage Lodge Horticultural Centre or the Roger Harvey Garden Centre, which also caters for younger visitors, with a childrens' corner. Old Stevenage about half a mile north has retained its wide tree-lined High Street with a green and some former coaching inns. Writer E. M. Forster (1879–1970) lived here as a child and the town features in some of his work.

As the A1(M) sweeps above to head east, open country, hitherto confined to brief interludes, becomes a permanent feature as the train passes the villages of Little Wymondley (L) and Great Wymondley (R) on its way to **Hitchin**, a lovely Hertfordshire town on the River Hiz. On Saturdays the market-place presents a lively and colourful scene with many stalls set up in the shadow of graceful St Mary's, the parish church; at Paynes Park an interesting collection reflecting local social history has been assembled and together with paintings forms an admirable art gallery and museum. A description in the limited space available here would be a disservice, and one must really explore on foot the old-world streets and alleys, lined with buildings whose irregular façades spanning centuries of history will delight the eye of artist and photographer.

Beyond Hitchin the main line continues by way of Peterborough while a branch diverges to Cambridge, both of which are described in *East Anglia by Rail*. The First Garden City Museum at Letchworth has been referred to earlier, but if you are continuing towards Cambridge you might also consider breaking your journey at Royston to visit the Cave, a bell-shaped cavity discovered in the eighteenth century and decorated with a series of religious carvings which might have been made by a medieval hermit.

The Moorgate Branch

At **Moorgate**, inner suburban trains use platforms integrated with the Underground station. The former City and South London (now Northern Line) surface building of 1900 is in red brick, with decorative stonework. The adjacent Metropolitan Railway station, opened in 1865, is served by London Underground Circle and Metropolitan lines, and by peak-hour BR services from the Bedford line (page 44). Above ground, the station was completely rebuilt in the 1970s as part of a development of offices and shops. Running north from Moorgate in twin tube tunnels, the Great Northern line serves three subterranean stations before surfacing at Drayton Park. **Old Street**, also served by Northern Line Underground trains, is close to John Wesley's Chapel in City Road. Opened in 1778, this fine building draws large numbers of pilgrims who also come to see Wesley's house, his tomb and the Museum of Methodism. Across the road in Bunhill Fields are the graves of other non-conformist figures such as Blake, Bunyan and Watts.

Essex Road, on the edge of Islington, was formerly known as Canonbury & Essex Road and until BR took over the station some of the platform seats still carried this name. At **Highbury & Islington** there is cross-platform interchange with Victoria Line services and the station is also served by Richmond–North Woolwich trains. The line surfaces at **Drayton Park** station, where the electricity supply system changes from third rail, used in the tube section, to the overhead wires used on the rest of the route. Trains used on Moorgate services are dual-voltage, and the pantographs are raised or lowered at Drayton Park. An area of derelict land (L) used to be occupied by the Northern Line car sheds when this line was part of the Underground network. About a quarter of a mile beyond Drayton Park station we join the main line from King's Cross near Finsbury Park.

The Hertford Loop

The double-track Hertford Loop leaves the main line just north of Alexandra Palace station and rejoins it just south of Stevenage. Reaching open country about ten miles from London, its surroundings are then almost completely rural until approaching the outskirts of Stevenage. The first station on the loop is **Bowes Park**, in an area of terraced and semi-detached houses, where the line crosses over the North Circular Road. The New River, cut in the seventeenth-century to provide the City of London with a new water supply, then runs alongside (R) for a short distance before curving away as the train approaches **Palmers Green**. Further suburban stations follow at

Winchmore Hill and at **Grange Park**, where serried ranks of villas begin a retreat in the face of distant green hills (L) and woodland at Bush Hill Park (R). Tower blocks loom ahead as the train nears **Enfield Chase**, one of two Network SouthEast stations with this suffix (the other is Wimbledon Chase). In this instance the word 'chase' signifies an area over which hunting rights belonged, by royal warrant, to private citizens as opposed to the king, whose hunting domain was 'forest' land. Conversion of chases to agricultural use contributed to the rise of foxhunting in eighteenth-century England.

The centre of Enfield (also served by Enfield Town station, page 60), is about half a mile away and still has something of the character of a country town, with a market place in front of the medieval parish church and the eighteenth-century houses of Gentleman's Row overlooking the New River and Chase Green Park. There is an art gallery and museum at Forty Hall, 1½ miles north of the town centre (page 60).

North of Enfield Chase the line runs on an embankment, with housing estates (L) and views (R) across Enfield and the Lea Valley to open country. Beyond **Gordon Hill** station, suburban housing is left behind: there are fields (L) and nurseries with extensive glasshouses (R) as the train approaches **Crews Hill**. It passes under the M25 and through a landscape of fields and woods before reaching a built-up area around **Cuffley** station. There is residential development (L) at Cuffley, and houses on the ridge (R) are at Goffs Oak. Leaving Cuffley, the train runs beside Cheshunt Common (R) before plunging into the 1½-mile-long Ponsbourne Tunnel to reach **Bayford** station which is comparatively isolated; the nearest villages are Bayford, half a mile to the west, and Brickendon, half a mile to the east. Extensive tracts of woodland, managed by the Woodland Trust and Hertfordshire County Council, are accessible to visitors. A special type of habitat, some areas have been designated Sites of Special Scientific Interest as, for example, Wormley Wood about 1½ miles away where among the distinctive flora and fauna of this ancient woodland you may stumble across one of the ubiquitous coal posts (page 106) beside an old road. Neighbouring Broxbourne Wood is chiefly coniferous, but with areas of grass and scrubland it has a variety of habitats. Do not be misled into thinking that Lea Valley line stations (pages 58–9) would be nearer – even Hoddesdon Park Wood away to the north-east is better reached from Bayford! Leaflets are available from tourist information centres for each site to help you make the most of a visit.

Continuing through open country to the outskirts of Hertford the line runs on embankments and viaducts crossing the rivers Lea and Mimram, a long-defunct line to Welwyn Garden City, and the A414 trunk road. There is a view (R) across the town centre, with the steeple of St Andrew's Church and the tower of All Saints' Church prominent as the train arrives at **Hertford North**. Although three-quarters of a mile away, the town centre is well worth a visit (Hertford East station, page 61, is however more convenient and offers an alternative, if scenically less attractive, route back to London).

For about five miles north of Hertford the railway runs close to the River Beane, flowing south to join the Lea. First seen (R) with houses crowning the hill beyond, as the train draws clear of Hertford North station, the Beane is bridged just before entering Molewood Tunnel and again after passing Waterford village. The train passes the site of Stapleford station (closed 1939) and approaches **Watton-at-Stone** in a cutting. The station, closed to passenger traffic in 1939, was rebuilt and reopened in response to local demand in 1982. The village (R) is between railway and river, but little can be seen from the station except a few houses and an oil depot alongside the line. For the next few miles the line runs on an embankment, with open country (L) and the Hertford–Stevenage Road close by (R) with fields and woods beyond. The outlying estates of Stevenage appear (R), boldly approaching close to the railway as it curves round to join the main line about a mile south of **Stevenage** station.

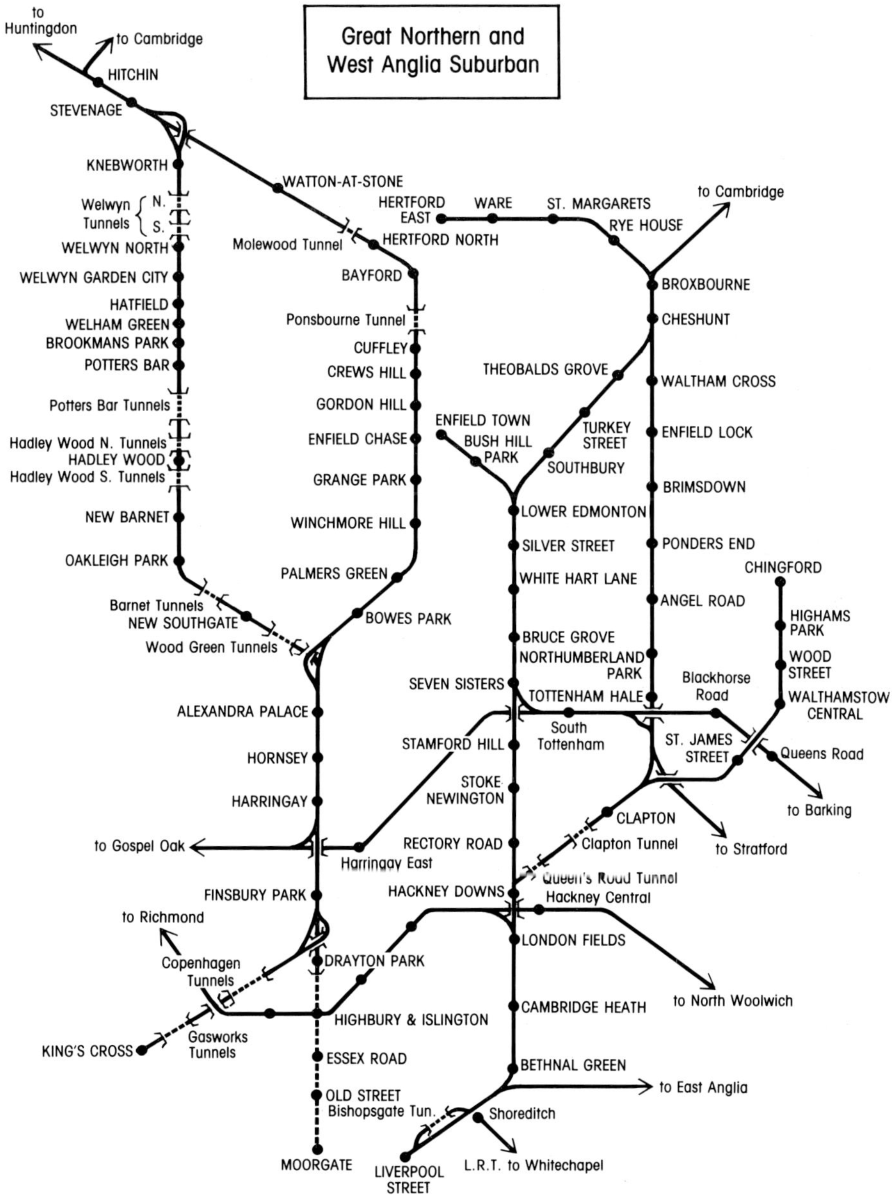

Great Northern and
West Anglia Suburban
to Huntingdon
to Cambridge
HITCHIN
STEVENAGE
KNEBWORTH
WATTON-AT-STONE
Welwyn Tunnels N. S.
WELWYN NORTH
Molewood Tunnel
HERTFORD NORTH
HERTFORD EAST
WARE
ST. MARGARETS
RYE HOUSE
to Cambridge
BROXBOURNE
CHESHUNT
WELWYN GARDEN CITY
BAYFORD
HATFIELD
WELHAM GREEN
BROOKMANS PARK
POTTERS BAR
Ponsbourne Tunnel
CUFFLEY
CREWS HILL
GORDON HILL
ENFIELD CHASE
GRANGE PARK
WINCHMORE HILL
PALMERS GREEN
BOWES PARK
Potters Bar Tunnels
Hadley Wood N. Tunnels
HADLEY WOOD
Hadley Wood S. Tunnels
NEW BARNET
OAKLEIGH PARK
Barnet Tunnels
NEW SOUTHGATE
Wood Green Tunnels
THEOBALDS GROVE
WALTHAM CROSS
ENFIELD TOWN
BUSH HILL PARK
TURKEY STREET
SOUTHBURY
ENFIELD LOCK
BRIMSDOWN
LOWER EDMONTON
SILVER STREET
WHITE HART LANE
PONDERS END
ANGEL ROAD
CHINGFORD
HIGHAMS PARK
WOOD STREET
WALTHAMSTOW CENTRAL
BRUCE GROVE
NORTHUMBERLAND PARK
SEVEN SISTERS
TOTTENHAM HALE
Blackhorse Road
South Tottenham
ST. JAMES STREET
Queens Road
to Barking
ALEXANDRA PALACE
HORNSEY
HARRINGAY
STAMFORD HILL
STOKE NEWINGTON
CLAPTON
Clapton Tunnel
to Stratford
to Gospel Oak
Harringay East
RECTORY ROAD
Queen's Road Tunnel
HACKNEY DOWNS
Hackney Central
FINSBURY PARK
to Richmond
LONDON FIELDS
Copenhagen Tunnels
DRAYTON PARK
to North Woolwich
HIGHBURY & ISLINGTON
CAMBRIDGE HEATH
KING'S CROSS
Gasworks Tunnels
ESSEX ROAD
BETHNAL GREEN
to East Anglia
OLD STREET
Bishopsgate Tun.
Shoreditch
MOORGATE
LIVERPOOL STREET
L.R.T. to Whitechapel

WEST ANGLIA SUBURBAN: LIVERPOOL STREET TO CHINGFORD, ENFIELD AND HERTFORD EAST

by Ian McGill

Liverpool Street station, opened in 1874 and now undergoing a major transformation, is the terminus for frequent electric trains to Chingford, Broxbourne (via Lea Valley line stations and Waltham Cross), and for Enfield Town, and Hertford East (via Lower Edmonton). Half-hourly weekday services (twenty minutes to Chingford) also apply on Sundays (when some stations are closed) to Enfield Town, but become hourly for Hertford, whilst Chingford is served every thirty minutes. Lea Valley stations are at present closed throughout weekends.

Negotiating the dreary approaches to Liverpool Street, Shoreditch LRT station may be glimpsed (R) and at **Bethnal Green** (page 101) the train veers away from the Norwich main line, passing inner suburban stations at **Cambridge Heath**, where narrow streets of terraced housing shut out the sun near the western extremity of Victoria Park (page 34). It crosses the Regent's Canal in dingy surroundings at South Hackney, served by **London Fields** station. The Richmond–North Woolwich line (page 29) passes below near **Hackney Downs** station, and Hertford and Enfield trains – whose route is described on page 59 – part company with those for Chingford and the Lea Valley, which tunnel their way to **Clapton** where the crowded inner suburbs, hesitating at the banks of the Lea, die away to allow an uninterrupted view over a landscape of marshland and reservoirs.

Trains for Broxbourne – a journey described below – and beyond diverge (L) at Clapton Junction leaving Chingford services to continue alone, crossing a freight line from Stratford on their way to Walthamstow, where **St James Street** is the first of three stations. Gospel Oak to Barking trains pass underneath, calling at Walthamstow Queens Road (R) as our train slows for **Walthamstow Central**, terminus of LRT's Victoria Line. **Wood Street** station is within half a mile of the lower end of Epping Forest, here a rather emasculated enclave hemmed in by suburbia. The little River Ching flows from a lake at **Highams Park** on the forest's western slopes, alongside Woodford golf course. Part of Epping Forest since 1891, the park originally belonged to an eighteenth-century mansion, Highams, which later became a school. There are no further stations along the remaining two miles to **Chingford** where Epping Forest, reaching almost to the station, has effectively checked the outward spread of London. Once a popular goal for East Enders enjoying a day in the country, the forest is still a place of peace and solitude. Queen Elizabeth's Hunting Lodge, a half-timbered building housing a forest museum, was built by Henry VIII for use by royal hunting parties. Lawrence of Arabia owned Pole Hill, and on its summit are two pillars nineteen feet apart, marking two Greenwich meridians (page 68). The smaller pillar marks true zero degrees longitude as adopted in 1851 whilst its companion, the Chingford Pillar, stands on the line of an earlier prime meridian defined in the eighteenth century. Interestingly, Ordnance Survey maps are still based on this earlier data.

From Clapton Junction, trains for Broxbourne via Waltham Cross reach the Lea Valley at Coppermill Junction, joining a goods line from Stratford (R) to cross an area of marsh and reservoirs before passing under the Gospel Oak–Barking line, to which it throws off a spur (L), and reaching **Tottenham Hale** which is also served by Victoria Line Underground trains. Like the remaining stations to Cheshunt and Ware it offers access to the Lea Valley Park (tel. 0992 717711), a major leisure facility which extends northwards from Leyton. At **Northumberland Park**, the Victoria Line depot

(R) occupies part of Tottenham Marsh, where in its early days Tottenham Hotspur Football Club played on a public pitch, storing its equipment at the station. Beyond, a narrow industrial belt extends up the valley, a legacy of the 1914–18 conflict when it became a centre of war industries. **Angel Road** is the nearest station to Banbury Reservoir, with its popular sailing centre for both novices and more experienced hands. A long-defunct line diverged (L) to Lower Edmonton, and continuing through a mainly industrial environment, trains reach **Ponders End** some two miles later, near the site of a government shell factory. Epping Forest crowns a distant wooded ridge (R) towards Chingford, becoming more prominent as we draw near to **Brimsdown**, which serves the Enfield Highway district. The wooded heights (R) recede as we cross the New River near **Enfield Lock**, but do not be tempted to alight here for Enfield town which is some 2½ miles away. The Royal Small Arms and Royal Gunpowder factories were established on land bordering the Lea (R) as we continue to **Waltham Cross** station (formerly Waltham Cross & Abbey), a nondescript modern building in mediocre surroundings where London meets with neighbouring Essex and Hertfordshire.

Waltham Cross, in Hertfordshire, is a short walk from the station via a subway and has a covered shopping precinct alongside which a rare gallows sign, spanning the High Street, survives from the old Four Swans Inn. A few yards away stands one of three surviving original Eleanor Crosses. Twelve such monuments were erected by Edward I at the places where the body of his Queen, Eleanor of Castile, rested on its journey from Lincolnshire to Westminster Abbey in 1290. This richly decorated cross has been much restored; there are others at Geddington and Northampton, but that at Charing Cross (page 77) in London is merely a Victorian replica. Waltham Abbey, the adjoining gardens, and the countryside centre at Hayes Hill and Abbey Farms midway along the Lea Valley Park are best reached by bus (route 242 and others). Officially the Abbey and Parish Church of Holy Cross and St Lawrence at Waltham Holy Cross in Essex, this is one of our finest surviving Norman churches and should on no account be missed. Filled with relics, this magnificent place of worship, probable burial place of King Harold, stands on the site of a medieval Augustinian priory of which little remains. The town, with its pedestrianised shopping area, is worth exploring, too, if you have time. In a few moments the train reaches **Cheshunt** where the Churchbury loop (page 60) converges (L).

Enfield and Hertford trains meander from Hackney Downs Junction through stations at **Rectory Road**, **Stoke Newington**, and **Stamford Hill** to cross the Gospel Oak–Barking line (whose station at South Tottenham is nearby) where a chord comes in (R) at **Seven Sisters**, named for seven elm trees which once stood in the locality. A branch used to diverge (L) to Palace Gates, near Alexandra Palace (page 52), but the only interchange facilities now available are with Victoria Line trains. Like Seven Sisters, **Bruce Grove** station in Tottenham is well placed for good local shopping facilities. Alight here also for Bruce Castle Park in Lordship Lane, where an excellent museum devoted to the Middlesex Regiment also has extensive exhibits related to both local and postal history (tel. 081 808 8772). **White Hart Lane** has been synonymous with football since Tottenham Hotspur Football Club, named after Shakespeare's fiery Harry Hotspur, moved here early this century. North Middlesex Hospital can be seen (L) at Upper Edmonton near **Silver Street** station, which is alongside attractive Pymmes Park where Elizabethan statesman Lord Burghley lived.

Picketts Lock Centre provides for a wide range of sporting activities, and although the Lea Valley line passes much closer it lacks a really convenient station, so it is advisable to alight at **Lower Edmonton** and take bus W8. There is little evidence of a short spur (R) from Angel Road, but Bury Street, a village overwhelmed by suburbia, is recalled in the name of a junction where Hertford trains diverge (R) – the journey to Hertford is described on page 60 – leaving those for Enfield to continue by way of

Bush Hill Park to terminate at **Enfield Town**. A plaque in the booking hall records that the first station on this site was adapted from a seventeenth-century mansion where Benjamin Disraeli's father was born and the poet Keats was educated. On Thursdays and Saturdays a bustling general market is held under the terms of a charter granted by James I in 1619. Gentleman's Row has several sixteenth- and seventeenth-century houses; Charles Lamb stayed here before renting Westwood Cottage at 89 Chase Side. Enfield Chase station on the Great Northern line (page 56) some three-quarters of a mile away offers an alternative route back to London.

From Bury Street Junction, Hertford trains take the line to Cheshunt which, like the Hainault Loop (page 102) was an over-optimistic attempt by the old Great Eastern Railway to stimulate suburban development, which in the event proved disappointing. Apart from a brief resurgence during the First World War, passenger services ceased in 1909 leaving the line to sink into limbo until reawakened in 1960 by electrification. **Southbury** station, known before as Churchbury, is closer to Ponders End than the Lea Valley station Ponders End, and during its period of closure was used to store building supplies. A temporary halt was opened for war workers in 1916 at Carterhatch Lane, midway towards the next station at **Turkey Street**. Serving Enfield Wash, this was originally known as Forty Hill and following closure became a private residence. White Webbs Park covers a large area to the west, beyond the former hamlet of Turkey Street. Forty Hall, built in 1629 for the then Lord Mayor of London, is now a local history museum. An untidy landscape follows, where scruffy pasture interspersed with housing has replaced market gardens. **Theobalds Grove**, also a residence during its period of disuse, is between Waltham Cross and Theobalds Park. Built by Elizabethan statesman William Cecil, Theobalds was later acquired by James I who replaced the original house with four smaller dwellings of which one, Old Palace House, survived until 1968. Sir Christopher Wren's massive Temple Bar of 1672, which stood in Fleet Street, was in 1887 moved here where it forms an impressive entrance. Cedars Park (entrance in Theobalds Lane near the station) belonged to Old Palace House but is now open to all.

In a few moments the Lea Valley route is joined (R) near **Cheshunt**, which was the centre of a thriving horticultural industry until the nurserymen were driven out by soaring land values, leaving little evidence except a legacy of rotting glasshouses scattered along the next few miles. Alight at **Broxbourne** for the Lido, where you can swim and relax in a simulated South Seas environment, and in summer sunbathe on the riverside terrace, watching at close quarters the boating activity which you may have seen from the train. You can hire vessels or join a waterbus trip at the boat centre, make a guided tour of Nazeing Glassworks (tel. 0992 464485), take the family along to Paradise Park and Woodland Zoo (tel. 0992 440494), or browse in Lowewood Museum, with its displays of local history, which is in a Georgian building dating from about 1750.

Overshadowed by the gargantuan form of Broxbourne Power Station, the train swings away from the Cambridge Line (R), and skirting Hoddesdon slows down for **Rye House**, where an unsuccessful plot to assassinate King Charles II was to have been carried out in 1683. Turn right out of the station, and almost at once the dreary surroundings melt away by the Lea. Opposite the delightful Rye House pub a bird sanctuary, open at weekends, has been created at Rye House Marsh Reserve adjacent to the gatehouse which is all that remains of Rye House, whose chequered history goes back to 1443 when it was built by Sir Andrew Ogard. Sandwiched between the Lea and New rivers, the train makes its way to **St Margarets** station, at the west end of Stanstead Abbots village. A branch to Buntingford (closed in 1964) diverged (R) near Great Amwell, its church peering quizzically through the trees (L) as the train continues towards **Ware**, whose one platform station stands on a short stretch of single track.

The gatehouse of Rye House (*Photo:* I. McGill)

Nuns at a local Carmelite monastery make the wafers used in celebrating Holy Communion, producing 2,500 hosts each day. Armed with a copy of the leaflet 'A Walk Around Ware', take time to see this thriving town, through which passed Roman Ermine Street and where Jane Dudley (Lady Jane Grey) was proclaimed Queen in 1553, only to be deposed nine days later by Mary I. The Great Bed of Ware, a massive four-poster dating from about 1580 and the largest bed in Britain, mentioned in Shakespeare's *Twelfth Night*, eventually found a new home at London's Victoria and Albert Museum, but two unusual features which may still be visited merit special mention. Scott's Grotto, created by eighteenth-century Quaker poet John Scott, is a series of passages linking six underground rooms, each intricately decorated with shells and flints. Opening is restricted, there is no illumination and visitors must bring a torch (tel. 0920 4131). In contrast, the premises of Concrete Utilities Limited, Great Amwell, have some 150 columns, lanterns and smaller artefacts which have been assembled and restored at the Museum of Street Lighting, providing an illuminating insight into an amenity which we take for granted. Entrance is free, but by appointment only (tel. 0920 2770).

Negotiating a level-crossing the train passes through an area of unkempt paddocks overshadowed by a low ridge (L) to reach the terminus at **Hertford East**, which is the better situated of the county town's two stations and where several features are worth noting. A single-track spur to the Great Northern Railway at Hertford North (page 56) passed behind the signal-box, whose adjacent searchlight signals are of London & North Eastern Railway vintage. Rather plain platform canopies and valancing contrast with etched glazing and an elaborate ceiling in the booking hall, but the finest feature is a *porte-cochère* where carriages deposited their passengers dry-shod.

An alternative return route is available from Hertford North.

HERTFORD

by Ian McGill

Hertford is the county town situated in the Lea (or Lee) Valley where in Saxon times the river could be forded near its confluence with the Beane, Rib and Mimram. In more recent times the Lea & Stort Navigation was an important commercial artery, but it now offers many miles of cruising for pleasure, and sport for anglers.

A good place to start a visit is the friendly tourist information centre, which provides a fund of essential information at Hertford Castle, set in attractive riverside parkland and successor to a Norman stronghold whose remains can still be seen. If you arrive at Hertford East station, on your way along Railway Street notice the Friends Meeting House, the oldest purpose-built place of Quaker worship in the world, near a modern shopping precinct at Bircherley Green. Sport and recreational facilities can be found at Hartham Common, where each Spring Bank Holiday the fair comes to town. Twice-weekly cattle markets still take place and a busy general market is held every Saturday.

Among the streets of elegant houses, shops and picturesque cottages are some with plasterwork of a typical East Anglian style known as pargeting. North of the town, Bengeo has an unspoilt Norman church dating from about 1120, which contains a Saxon window and thirteenth-century wall paintings. County Hall, in contrast, was built in 1939 in Scandinavian style and is an interesting departure from the architecture often associated with civic buildings. Paper was first made in Britain at Sele Mill, on the Beane, in 1488 by John Tate. A successor to this mill, now derelict, can be seen on the way to the town from Hertford North station, where an embankment beside the Sele Arms carried a defunct line from Hertford East.

The purity of local water is responsible for the enviable reputation enjoyed by products of the local brewery. McMullens, one of a diminishing number of independent breweries, has produced beer in Hertford for over 150 years, and despite the introduction of modern equipment still relies on traditional methods of brewing. In 1891 the brewery moved to its present site in Hartham Lane; its distinctive clock tower pre-dates the brewery by about thirty years, and is thought to have come from Wormwood Scrubs Prison.

Christ's Hospital School for Girls in Fore Street was founded in 1683 as a branch of the earlier boys' school, started by Edward VI in 1552. Popularly known as the Blue Coat School because of the boys' uniforms, it was originally a foundling hospital in the City of London which went on to become a seat of learning. Eventually the boys' school moved to Horsham and the girls came here to Hertford.

There are so many lovely villages hidden deep in the surrounding countryside that to single out just a few might seem unjust, but if one has to choose then perhaps Westmill in springtime would be a favourite, although this is not to deny the charms of neighbours such as Braughing, Ardeley and the Hadhams. However, if you decide to explore further afield you will need to bring your cycle, or be fully conversant with current bus timetables in order to make the best use of your time.

Hertford Castle (*Photo:* I. McGill)

THE DOCKLANDS LIGHT RAILWAY

by Tim Young

Opened by the Queen and Prince Philip on 30 July 1987, the Docklands Light Railway operates over 12.1 km of route and serves fifteen stations. Branches from Tower Gateway in the City and Stratford in east London unite at West India Quay, Poplar, to pursue a course down the centre of the Isle of Dogs, reaching a terminus at Island Gardens on the north bank of the Thames opposite Greenwich, to which it is connected by pedestrian tunnel. Built jointly by the London Docklands Development Corporation and London Regional Transport, it is a segregated automatic high-frequency passenger carrying system, mostly elevated above ground level, and although driverless each train has a 'Train Captain' aboard for revenue protection and security reasons. Stations have a public address system, closed-circuit TV surveillance and lift access for disabled passengers. Tickets may be purchased in bulk at local newsagents, or singly from station vending machines, and through booking facilities are available with stations on the Underground network. Trains normally consist of two cars, but the system has been so phenomenally successful that stations are being extended to cope with longer trains, and two privately financed extensions are already planned, eastwards to Beckton and westwards to Bank. Trains operate every 7½ minutes between Tower Gateway/Stratford and West India Quay, and every 3¾ minutes thence to Island Gardens.

A port since Roman times with access to the sea via the River Thames, London's riverbanks were crowded with wharves and warehouses, especially in the vicinity of the Tower of London. By the end of the eighteenth century there was clearly a need for a proper system of enclosed docks, and the first of these was opened on the Isle of Dogs in 1802 by the West India Docks Company. Others followed, the most controversial being St Katherine Docks in 1825, involving demolition of 1,250 homes. Thirty

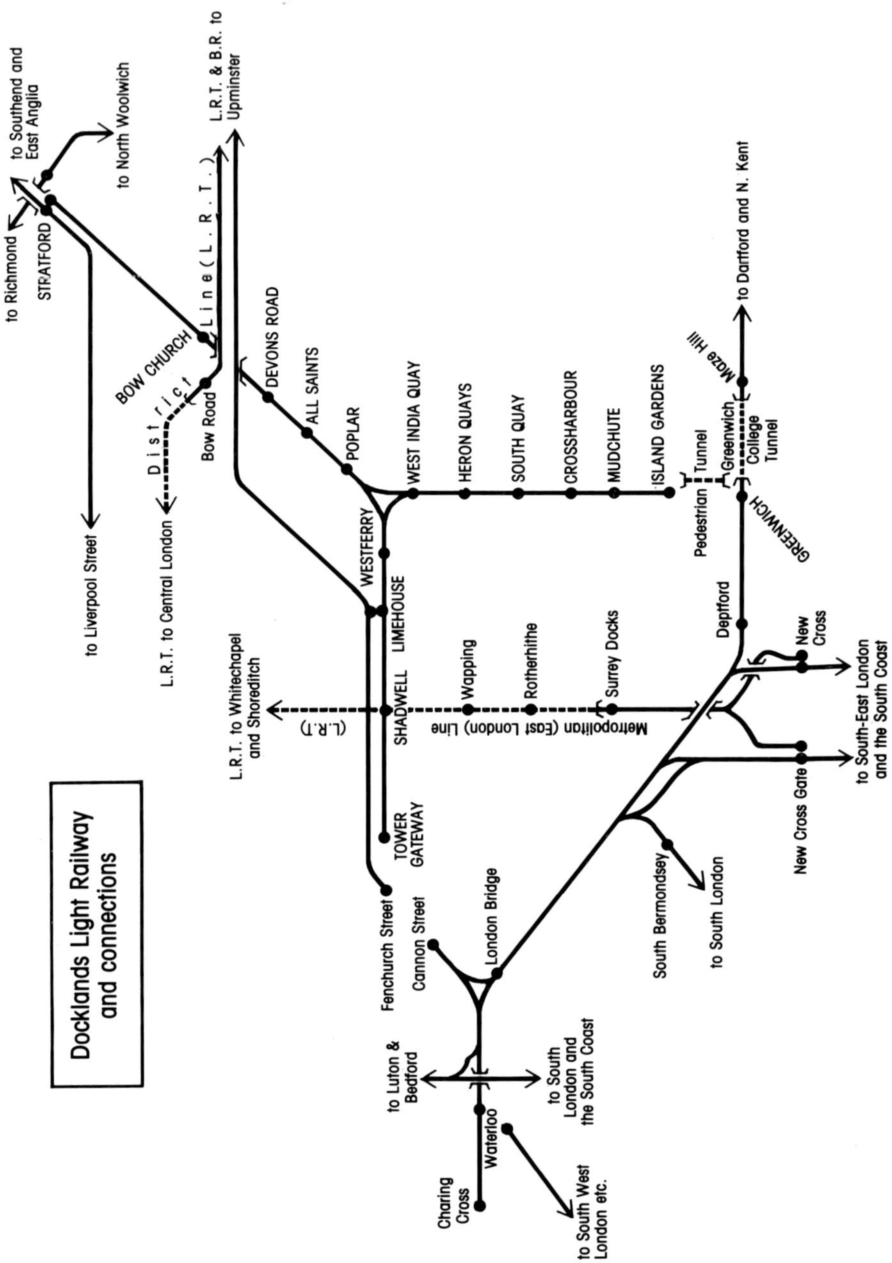

Docklands Light Railway and connections

years later the Royal Victoria Dock, downriver from its predecessors and intended specifically for steamships, opened, followed by the 1¾-mile-long Royal Albert Dock which could accommodate the largest ships then afloat. Finally in 1921 King George V Dock, named in honour of the reigning monarch, was commissioned and this, too, could handle the most modern shipping.

Decline began during the Second World War, when the risk of enemy action at sea and bomb damage to the docks themselves conspired to reduce traffic. Mechanisation later led to a steady reduction in the workforce, and the older docks could not handle post-war shipping; thus in 1967 East India Dock became the first to close. The others gradually followed, and today all commercial freight activity has ceased.

In the 1970s a decision was taken to regenerate the area, and improved public transport was seen as a prime necessity. Anticipated traffic levels made the bus an impracticable solution, an Underground extension was ruled out by cost, and so a form of light railway was decided upon; this would use some of the many abandoned railway routes in the area, thus reducing construction costs. To describe the route is in many respects a pointless task as the area is in a state of ferment with new buildings and other changes to the scene occurring almost daily, but I shall endeavour to describe some of the more permanent and interesting features.

From **Tower Gateway**, where access is by escalator inside a round glass tower, the line follows the course of the former London & Blackwall Railway, built in 1840. As the train moves silently away, look back (R) to see the Tower of London, with its familiar White Tower. This ancient fortress, which houses the Crown Jewels, attracts millions of visitors each year who also see the armoury, beefeaters, ravens and Traitors' Gate. It is across the road from Tower Gateway, and a pedestrian walkway also links the DLR with Tower Hill Underground station. Fenchurch Street station (page 73) can be seen (L) as the train accelerates, and new construction work (R) is part of the extension to Bank station. Passing through drab surroundings in company with BR trains (L) we pause at **Shadwell**, an interchange with the East London section of the Metropolitan Line. At **Limehouse** there is an interchange with BR trains, which veer away (L) as we cross Limehouse Viaduct, spanning the Regent's

The Tower of London (*Photo:* H. Atkinson)

Canal, towards **Westferry**, where the adjacent Dockmaster's House of 1807 now serves as offices. Climbing steeply to head south into dockland, the train negotiates a triangular junction with the branch from Stratford (L) to arrive at **West India Quay**.

Passengers from **Stratford** will find DLR trains at platform 4, overlooking an industrial landscape of factories and railway installations. Central Line trains disappear hurriedly underground (R), but BR trains persevere for rather longer before leaving us at Bow Junction, where our train curves away (L) and drops steeply to join the old North London Railway route (R) from Victoria Park. **Bow Church**, our first station stop, is handy for Bow Road Underground station. After passing the former NLR works (L) and heading under BR lines from Fenchurch Street the train arrives at **Devons Road**. Alight here for the unusual Gas Museum, illustrating, with special reference to London, the history of this essential industry; telephone 071 987 2000 for opening times. Limehouse Cut follows as the train passes through an area which has experienced intense industrial activity, to reach **All Saints**. The line swings west alongside the DLR depot (R) and **Poplar** station is close to the new Billingsgate Fish Market (L), an impressive new building displaying large badges on red brick walls and sheltering beneath pyramids of yellow roof girders, with distinctive fish-shaped weather vanes at each end. Climbing away to join the Tower Gateway branch, the train negotiates a triangular junction (R) to arrive at **West India Quay**.

From here onwards there are some spectacular views, beginning with a lofty crossing of the West India Docks (Import) to reach Canary Quay and the site of a future station at Canary Wharf. Of the remaining warehouses, number 31 is home of Limehouse Studios and number 30 is bisected by DLR trains, which then glide above the old Export Dock to reach **Heron Quays**. Looking down on the waters of South West India Dock you may see a few vessels of the Maritime Trust at their moorings before the line curves around between the British Telecom Business Centre (L) and the Enterprise Business Park (R). At **South Quay** a tall black building (L) is the new home of the *Daily Telegraph*. The train then crosses the Millwall Cut, heading south to reach **Crossharbour**, where a large ASDA Superstore has proved very popular in an area not well endowed with shops. Alight here also for the London Docklands Visitors Centre, and find out more about this fascinating area and its phenomenal transformation during recent years.

Flanked by Millwall Docks (R), a farm and park have been established (L) on land beyond East Ferry Road at **Mudchute**. This station got its name after a pneumatic dredger was devised in the 1880s by a Mr Duckham, the Dock Engineer, to overcome silting in Millwall Dock; the mud was transferred by pipeline and deposited on a site known as the 'Mudchute'. Operations ceased in 1904 and the site is now parkland. From the front seat of the train there is an unrivalled view over the river to Greenwich and the twin towers of the National Maritime Museum, as we embark on the last leg of the journey looking down on a park (L) which was home of Millwall Football Club until 1910 when it moved south across the Thames.

Island Gardens terminus is approached across Millwall Park Viaduct, built in 1872 to carry the single-track Millwall Extension Railway, part of an extensive dock railway system, to a waterfront terminus at North Greenwich; these passenger services ceased in 1926. During the last war, some of the arches were used as an air-raid shelter but now house a DLR shop and information point where you can obtain a copy of *Travelling Light*, the railway's own excellent 'where to go and what to see' guide which deals far more comprehensively with the local scene than is possible here. This is the end of the journey on Britain's newest railway which, with its modern trains and striking stations serving a revitalised area, has risen phoenix-like from the ashes of railways long since given up as outmoded by previous generations.

Across Saunders Ness Road, Island Gardens, opened in 1859, look enviously towards Greenwich, which is accessible through a foot tunnel under the river.

The clipper *Cutty Sark*, preserved at Greenwich

GREENWICH

by Alison Hunter

Closely associated for centuries with British maritime history and a favourite home of sovereigns, Greenwich has much of interest for its visitors. Only a few minutes' journey by direct train from London, the town may also be approached across the park from neighbouring stations at Maze Hill and Blackheath, or you can travel by Docklands Light Railway to Island Gardens and walk through a pedestrian tunnel under the Thames to emerge in the shadow of the graceful clipper *Cutty Sark*. Safely berthed in a dry dock, she was built on the Clyde and launched at Dumbarton in 1869 for the China tea trade, but achieved fame later for her speed when engaged on the Australian wool run. Sold to a Portugese owner in 1895, the vessel eventually returned to this country and lay moored at Greenhithe before moving to Greenwich for preservation in 1954. Her figurehead represents Burns' 'Nannie', clad in a chemise, a loose-fitting garment after which the ship is named. *Gipsy Moth IV*, berthed nearby, was the first yacht to be raced single-handed around the world, a feat accomplished in 226 days by Francis Chichester in 1966. On his return he was knighted by the Queen in a televised ceremony from Greenwich.

A riverside promenade starting at Greenwich Pier runs past the impressive Royal Naval College, which stands on the site of the Tudor Greenwich Palace which had fallen into disrepair. Although Charles II started to rebuild the palace at Greenwich, it was never again used as a royal residence. Work began in 1694, but was not completed until 1760 when it became the Royal Naval Hospital; it became the Royal Naval College in 1873. The buildings are the work of several eminent architects, including Wren and Hawksmoor. The magnificently decorated Painted Hall, open to visitors, is considered a masterpiece to rival the Sistine Chapel.

Standing at the edge of Greenwich Park, the National Maritime Museum occupies three elegant buildings, linked by colonnades. The central building, the Queen's House, is a Palladian-style villa built by Inigo Jones for Queen Anne, wife of James I. Among its distinguished features is a spiral or 'tulip' staircase. The east and west wings date from 1807 and commemorate the Battle of Trafalgar. Within is a museum, the largest of its kind in the world, which comprehensively covers every aspect of ships and seafaring activity, including a very fine collection of paintings and models.

Greenwich Park covers 200 acres of hillside overlooking the Thames and was emparked by royal licence in 1433. The first of England's royal parks to be enclosed, it was stocked with deer to provide sport. It assumed its present formal appearance, with planned tree planting, during the seventeenth century. James I replaced the park's fencing with a twelve-foot-high brick wall some two miles long, much of which still stands. A magnificent rose garden adjoins Chesterfield House, which last century became the park ranger's residence. Paths climb steeply up to the Old Royal Observatory from which there are superb views. Charles II commissioned Sir Christopher Wren to build the observatory, now known as Flamsteed House in honour of the first Astronomer Royal. His successor, Edmund Halley, discovered the comet of that name, and subsequent holders of the post continued to live here until 1948 when the Royal Observatory moved to Hurstmonceux Castle in Sussex, although part of its work had already been transferred to a remote location in Surrey.

Today Flamsteed House is a museum with an extensive collection of astronomical and timekeeping instruments. A timeball, probably the oldest time signal, was erected on the roof in 1833 as a means of distributing Greenwich Mean Time, now universally used for timekeeping and navigation by land, sea and air. At 12.55 p.m. each day the ball is hoisted half-way up the pole and three minutes later it moves to the top, ready to drop at precisely 1 p.m., activated by a 24-hour clock at the courtyard gates. Nearby are standard measures of length and the famous meridian line, where you can stand astride eastern and western hemispheres. Originally defined in the eighteenth century, revised calculations in 1851 by the then Astronomer Royal Sir George Airy produced the present Greenwich Meridian, zero degrees longitude, which has been the world's prime meridian since its adoption in 1884 as the basis for international time reckoning. A few paces away stands a statue of General Wolfe who lived at Macartney House, and who embarked at Greenwich for Canada and the Battle of Quebec. Elegant houses overlook the park from Crooms Hill, one of London's oldest thoroughfares, where there is an unusual museum devoted entirely to fans and fan-making (tel. 081 305 1441). When you have savoured the walks and views and marvelled at the art and architecture of this historic corner of London, you can browse in the shops or pause for rest and refreshment at a local tavern or restaurant before taking the train back to town.

LONDON-BY-THE-SEA: VARIOUSLY TO SOUTHEND, ALSO SOUTHMINSTER AND SHOEBURYNESS

by Philip Harrison, John Morley and Tim Young

Southend is served from two London termini: a fast frequent train service runs from Liverpool Street to Southend Victoria, and an alternative route from Fenchurch Street goes to Southend Central and on to Shoeburyness.

Liverpool Street has a high percentage of commuters travelling to work in London among its daily passengers, but because the station is being drastically redeveloped we shall refrain from looking around. A maze of temporary walkways have to be negotiated to reach the train, which slinks through a tunnel before running past the deserted platforms of Bishopsgate station, closed in 1916. Leaving the main line to Cambridge and beyond (L) at **Bethnal Green** (page 101), the train crosses the Grand Union Canal and passes the sites of other defunct stations at Globe Road and Coborn Road, among dingy factories and typical inner-city housing, to reach Bow Junction, where the Docklands Light Railway (page 63) runs alongside (R).

Three more waterways are bridged along the remaining mile to **Stratford**, a major freight terminal and busy interchange between BR services and those of the Central Line and DLR. After a short journey the train reaches **Maryland** (formerly Maryland Point), a rather drab little station rebuilt, as were several others, in 1946 when the line was electrified. Beyond **Forest Gate**, another East End suburban station, a spur runs off (R) to join the Gospel Oak–Barking line, whose station at Woodgrange Park is not far away, to provide a link with the Fenchurch Street routes. **Manor Park** station lies at the edge of Wanstead Flats, between the large Manor Park and City of London cemeteries (L), before trains cross the River Roding to reach **Ilford**, where a large electric multiple unit depot (L) obscures the site of a former spur to Newbury Park (page 102). This is quickly followed by stations at **Seven Kings** and **Goodmayes**, before suburbia loosens its grip near **Chadwell Heath**, where a fourteeen-foot-tall obelisk at the lineside is a coal dues marker (page 106).

At **Romford**, with its brewery and stadium close by (L), we briefly interrupt the journey to Southend (which is continued on page 71), for this is the junction for a short three-mile branch to Upminster which was built in 1893 by the London, Tilbury & Southend Railway to stop the rival Great Eastern Railway from reaching Tilbury. Trains leave at half-hourly intervals (weekdays only) from a bay platform (number 1) on the 'up' side and after a few hundreds yards the recently electrified single track curves away (R) through an almost uninterrupted panorama of semi-detached suburbia. About halfway, trains pause at the only intermediate station, **Emerson Park**, opened in 1909 and recently rebuilt. Soon a fine white weatherboarded windmill (page 75) may be seen ahead among the buildings of **Upminster**, where, after running beside the Fenchurch Street and District lines, the train terminates at platform 6.

Some services once continued to Grays and Tilbury, but now passengers for these destinations must proceed to platform 1a, from where trains depart hourly on Mondays to Fridays and half-hourly on Saturdays, quickly veering away from the main line past Cranham (R) and across open country near tiny North Ockendon (L) to reach the only intermediate station, **Ockendon**. Serving South Ockendon, it has a loop enabling trains to pass on the single line, and is convenient for Grange Waters water-sports centre. A varying pattern of fields and industrial units follows until, after the train emerges from a cutting, the Proctor and Gamble factory appears (R), seen against the background of Purfleet Cement Works, as the train joins the Tilbury Loop

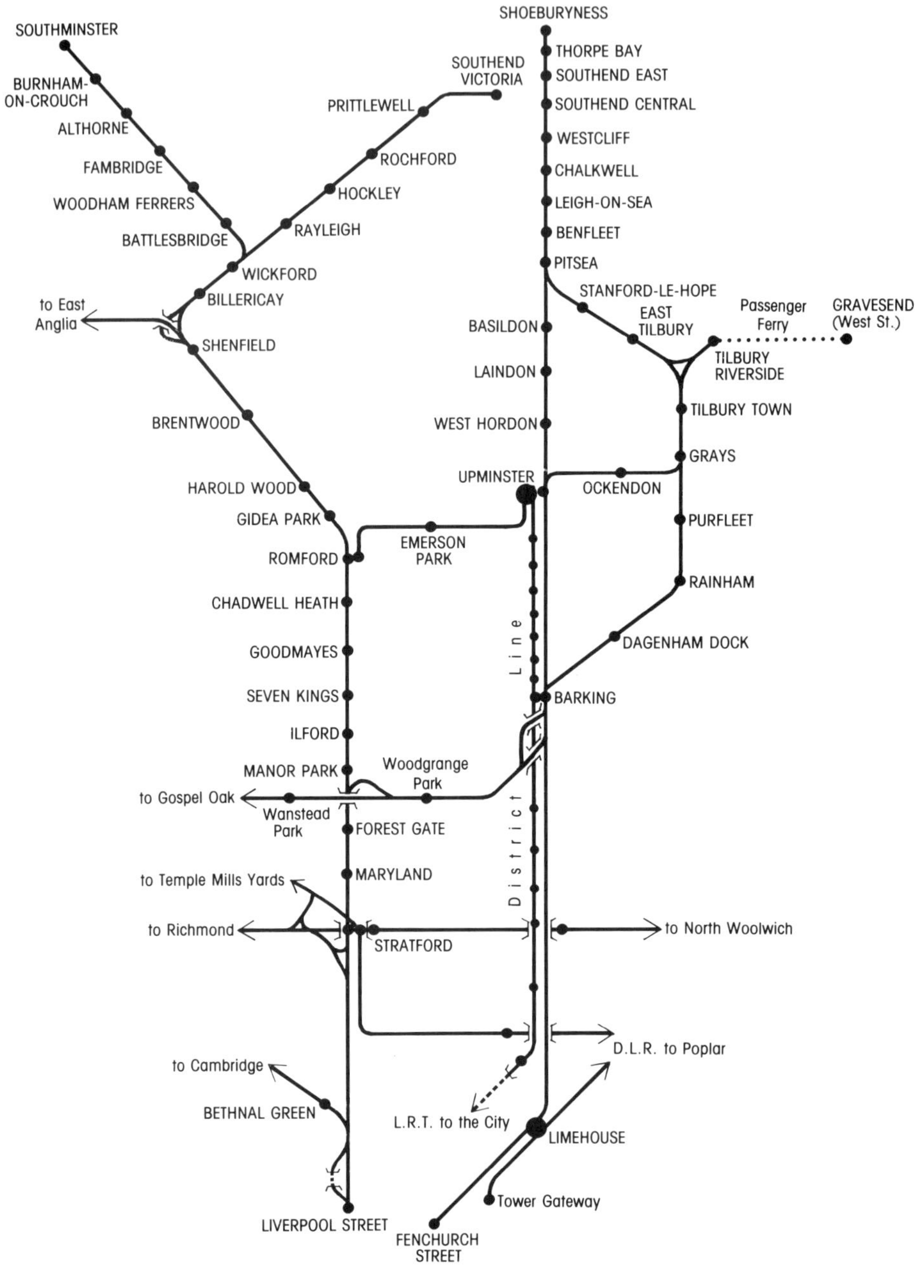

SOUTHMINSTER
BURNHAM-ON-CROUCH
ALTHORNE
FAMBRIDGE
WOODHAM FERRERS
BATTLESBRIDGE
WICKFORD
BILLERICAY
to East Anglia
SHENFIELD
BRENTWOOD
HAROLD WOOD
GIDEA PARK
ROMFORD
EMERSON PARK
CHADWELL HEATH
GOODMAYES
SEVEN KINGS
ILFORD
MANOR PARK
Woodgrange Park
to Gospel Oak
Wanstead Park
FOREST GATE
MARYLAND
to Temple Mills Yards
to Richmond
STRATFORD
to Cambridge
BETHNAL GREEN
LIVERPOOL STREET
SOUTHEND VICTORIA
PRITTLEWELL
ROCHFORD
HOCKLEY
RAYLEIGH
SHOEBURYNESS
THORPE BAY
SOUTHEND EAST
SOUTHEND CENTRAL
WESTCLIFF
CHALKWELL
LEIGH-ON-SEA
BENFLEET
PITSEA
STANFORD-LE-HOPE
EAST TILBURY
Passenger Ferry
GRAVESEND (West St.)
TILBURY RIVERSIDE
TILBURY TOWN
GRAYS
BASILDON
LAINDON
WEST HORDON
UPMINSTER
OCKENDON
PURFLEET
RAINHAM
DAGENHAM DOCK
District Line
BARKING
to North Woolwich
D.L.R. to Poplar
L.R.T. to the City
LIMEHOUSE
Tower Gateway
FENCHURCH STREET

at West Thurock Junction (R) near **Grays**. For the remainder of the journey to Tilbury Riverside, please turn to page 73.

Resuming at **Romford** the journey from Liverpool Street to Southend, inner suburban services finish at **Gidea Park** from where a cutting leads to **Harold Wood**, the last station in Greater London. Following the Weald Brook (L), the train climbs Brentwood Bank to enter Essex through a brief stretch of open country, a prelude to **Brentwood**. In Roman times this area was covered by dense forest which was 'brent' or burnt in order to make way for a settlement which was later used by pilgrims on their way to the shrine of St Thomas à Becket at Canterbury.

In the centre of modern Brentwood a granite obelisk commemorates William Hunter, who lived when Queen Mary was intent on restoring the Catholic faith to supremacy. Hunter and his vicar disagreed about matters of doctrine and the vicar had him arrested. The Bishop of London urged Hunter to recant his Protestant beliefs, but to no avail, and he was burnt at the stake. This memorial was built to his memory in 1861 and part of the tree where he was burned is still preserved at the Brentwood School museum. Outside the town, country estates at Weald Park and Thorndon Park have been set aside for public enjoyment. Great Warley has a remarkable art nouveau church, St Mary's, built in 1902–4.

A long, shallow cutting over Ingrave Summit brings the train to **Shenfield**, with its unusual parish church: as stone was not commonly found in Essex and was therefore expensive, the pillars and arches which line the aisle were made instead from solid oak! Here, just over twenty miles from London, the train dives under the main Norwich line and for the remainder of the journey traverses a branch opened in 1889 by the GER to obtain a share of the lucrative traffic to Southend, which until then had been carried by the London, Tilbury & Southend Railway and Thames steamships. After rejoining the 'up' lines which diverge separately, a four-mile run ensues through open country to **Billericay** station, in a wooded cutting at the north end of this busy and attractive country town. A local miller, Christopher Martin, was one of three men who chartered the *Mayflower* so that they and the Pilgrim Fathers might emigrate to New England. The Peasants' Revolt of 1381, led by Wat Tyler and provoked by a tyrannical government determined to impose an unpopular poll tax, was finally crushed at Norsey Wood, outside the town. Continuing through wooded country past Ramsden Bellhouse (R), impressive Rattenden church is visible (L) towards Battlesbridge and there are distant views across open country (R) towards Basildon.

Wickford is the junction for Southminster, branch trains leaving from a bay platform before bearing away (L) from the Southend line (the journey along which resumes on page 72) along a single track which follows the north bank of the River Crouch. Both routes celebrated their centenary in 1989, but this one is still very much a rural branch and is soon out in the country, crossing the Crouch to reach **Battlesbridge**, one of the quietest of Network SouthEast stations. A few minutes' walk away a sizeable antiques centre (open Wednesdays to Sundays) occupies a number of old buildings close to a bridge which marks the limit of river navigation. Rattenden church, two miles north, contains a thirty-foot-high monument of Italian marble, which commemorates Edward Humphrey who died in 1727.

It is only around the next station, **Woodham Ferrers**, that any significant change has occurred since the railway arrived. The small village which it served is on higher ground about a mile northward, but during the last fourteen years Essex County Council has transformed a scattered habitation of plotland bungalows near the railway into a new town, South Woodham Ferrers, which now has a population of about 15,000. An attractive and mostly traffic-free shopping area and civic centre are about fifteen minutes' walk away. A large influx of population has led to a corresponding increase in commuters, whose travel needs were met by reintroducing peak-hour through trains to and from Liverpool Street when the branch was electrified in 1986.

There are several level-crossings on the way to **Fambridge**, now the only place where trains can pass. North Fambridge lies just south of the railway, looking across the river towards its smaller neighbour, South Fambridge, on the opposite bank. **Althorne**, three miles further east, is the closest station to the Crouch and at the level-crossing a lane leads (L) to Althorne village and (R) to riverside salt marshes. Approaching **Burnham-on-Crouch** there is an excellent view over the yachting area, headquarters of the Royal Burnham, Royal Corinthian and other yacht clubs, before the scenery changes as the line forsakes the river. Burnham, until recent development at South Woodham the largest town on the branch, has a long street leading south from its station to reach High Street, and a short but attractive waterfront, whence lengthy walks may be taken along a riverside footpath. Across the Crouch can be seen the tower blocks of Southend-on-Sea, but no comparable buildings spoil the skyline of this small, peaceful riverside town.

The railway now turns north for the final two miles to **Southminster**, 16½ miles and thirty minutes' journey from Wickford; the visitor who walks the short distance from station to village centre cannot fail to notice the relative peace and quiet to be found at this end of the Dengie peninsula. Mangapps Farm Railway museum, about a mile from Burnham station on the Southminster road, is open every weekend from 1 to 6 p.m., and on Wednesday afternoons from Easter to September. Besides lesser relics and memorabilia, there is a small stud of steam and diesel locomotives behind which visitors can ride on a short demonstration track. Easy gradients and absence of heavy traffic make this an attractive area for cyclists and from Fambridge it is only six miles to the old and largely unspoilt town of Maldon, from where a further easy ride of ten miles will complete a circular tour to Southminster. Also ten miles away, but in a north-easterly direction beyond Bradwell-on-Sea, is the historic chapel of St Peter's-on-the-Wall, dating from the mid seventh century and by far the oldest church in Essex. For those without cycles, Maldon can be reached by bus from Burnham at hourly intervals on weekdays and every ninety minutes on Sundays, and together with a good train service is an encouragement to visitors to explore this forgotten corner of Essex.

Southend trains leave **Wickford** amid new development before reaching open country. After about three miles the A127 Southend Arterial Road (R) was the first new 'motor road' to be built after the First World War and is now one of the busiest in the country. Approaching **Rayleigh**, the church and windmill are prominent (R), the latter having been restored externally as part of a community centre. A steep walk to the town centre can be avoided by boarding a bus near the 'up'-side exit, but a pleasant approach on foot is via Rayleigh Mount (National Trust), the site of a castle which has been found to date from about 1086, and from which there are fine views. Four local men who were martyred in 1555 are remembered by a memorial in High Street. The railway begins to describe a semi-circle, overlooking the Crouch valley (L) on its way to **Hockley**, which once had visions of becoming a fashionable spa town. 'Matchbox' toys are produced by a factory (L) at **Rochford**, where the clubhouse, dating from 1548, of Rochford Hundred Golf Club is all that remains of Rochford Hall, home of Anne Boleyn. Crossing the River Roach, which gave the town its name, the train passes Southend Airport (R), on its way to **Prittlewell** where there are remains of an ancient priory. This is also the nearest station to Roots Hall, home of Southend United Football Club, but less well known is the fact that development at the 'south end' of Prittlewell, commenced in 1867, was the beginning of the present resort at **Southend-on-Sea**, where in half a mile our train terminates at **Victoria** station, adjacent to a shopping centre, bus station, and the town museum.

There are many shops along the pedestrianised High Street, which at about its mid point passes Southend Central station (R) before at its far end commanding a fine view across the Thames estuary to Sheerness in Kent. At low tide the river all but disappears, which is why the town boasts, at about 1⅓ miles, the longest pleasure pier in the world. Excursion vessels are able to berth at all states of the tide. You can walk, or ride by train, out to the pierhead for a closer view of the many ships passing to and from London's river. Southend is very commercialised and not the place for a quiet holiday, but with plenty to amuse and entertain all ages it is ideal for families.

There are quieter spots, as you may discover by reading about the alternative journey to Southend – this time from London's **Fenchurch Street** station. Opened in 1841 and hidden in a narrow side street, it has recently been renovated and the floodlit façade is impressive after dark.

Setting out past Tower Gateway (R), terminus of the Docklands Light Railway (page 63), which accompanies us at rooftop level over the East End, we drift through long-abandoned stations at Leman Street and Shadwell to **Limehouse** (formerly Stepney East) station, an interchange with DLR trains which then veer off (R). Across the Regent's Canal the site of another forgotten station is passed at Burdett Road before District Line services come alongside (L) at Campbell Road near Three Mills (L) (page 34) to call at a series of stations not served by BR trains, whose next stop is at **Barking**. Flyovers usher in trains from the Gospel Oak and Liverpool Street routes, which together with those of the District Line make this a major interchange station. If you are travelling by the direct route via Barking, please turn to page 74.

Trains running via Tilbury diverge (R) almost at once to traverse the heavily industrialised Thamesside levels, whose installations generate much of the freight traffic at the busy yards near **Dagenham Dock**, where the huge Ford Motor Company plant is prominent (R). Military firing ranges occupy marshes (R) around **Rainham** (not to be confused with its Kentish namesake). One of the few surviving areas of undeveloped Thamesside saltmarsh, a valuable haven for wetland flora and fauna including rare and protected species, it is designated a Site of Special Scientific Interest. At the time of writing, however, controversy rages over its future, prompted by recent proposals to create an extensive theme park and industrial sites. As the train crosses Mar Dyke, conspicuous oil storage tanks at **Purfleet** Lubricants Plant glisten like gigantic globules of frog spawn, and the new Dartford Bridge, still under construction, is seen (R). The Upminster branch (page 69) trails in (L) near **Grays**, and skirting docks and container depots (R) the train comes to **Tilbury Town** station. The journey from here to Southend resumes on page 74.

Passengers for **Tilbury Riverside** and the Gravesend passenger ferry should alight here and join trains from Upminster, which at once sweep away (R) for half a mile to reach a vast shabby terminus station cringing alongside the impressive London International Cruise Terminal (R). Not surprisingly perhaps, BR has announced a proposal to close Riverside station, a threat which if realised could seriously undermine the value of the ferry crossing for rail travellers. A suggestion that, in the event of closure, BR would seek to introduce a substitute bus service seems both unsatisfactory and irrelevant when a more sensible answer might be a drastic rationalisation, keeping just one or perhaps two platforms here, thus releasing most of this vast underused site for redevelopment, whilst still providing a train service. The ferry crossing is operated by Sealink British Ferries and provides a half-hourly service on weekdays (hourly on Sundays) with extra sailings at peak travel times. Passengers joining at Tilbury pay for their passage on disembarkation at Gravesend.

Overshadowed by a massive power station, Tilbury Fort (English Heritage), built by Henry VIII in 1670 to defend the Thames Estuary and later extended, is an outstanding example of seventeenth-century fortifications which is well worth visiting. A white weatherboarded pub, The World's End, once the ferry house, is nearby, and on a fine day the garden is a pleasant place to rest, but one can well imagine how appropriate a name it might seem on a wild, stormy night! Adjoining marshland provides a habitat for various bird species, including Brent geese and eider duck,

Tilbury Fort – the Water Gate (*Photo:* I. McGill)

which may be observed from paths following the riverbank downstream. Equipped to handle the largest container ships and bulk cargoes, Tilbury is the modern port of London, and the short ferry crossing to Kent offers an unrivalled panorama of maritime activity. From Gravesend (page 82) frequent trains provide an alternative route back to London.

It is necessary to retrace our steps to Tilbury Town to continue the original journey. Skirting the town (L) a direct line comes in (R) from Riverside, but as its use is now confined to rush hours it is of little benefit for most travellers. As the train passes through pastoral scenery, a level-crossing marks the site of Low Street station (closed 1967) and in a few moments the train arrives at **East Tilbury**, which serves a community which grew up around the Bata shoe factory of 1932 (R). Coalhouse Fort, another of the Thames estuary defences, contains a small museum and is occasionally open (tel. 0375 850484). Windswept marshes continue almost to **Stanford-le-Hope**, an agreeable little town which had the privilege of being served by the last London Transport country bus route to run on Christmas Day! Just before the station a branch leads off (R) to serve vast riverside oil refineries whilst our train proceeds through increasingly urban surroundings to rejoin the main line (L) at **Pitsea**. The description of the journey from here to Southend resumes on page 75.

From Barking, District Line trains continue (L) to accompany main line services, serving a further series of stations which have been relinquished by BR. Many people would probably dismiss Barking and its neighbour Dagenham as modern suburbs, but in fact this is merely the latest phase of a very long history. St Margaret's Church occupies the site of Barking Abbey, the greatest Benedictine nunnery in Britain of which there are still some remains. Fishing later became important and a distinctive type of local vessel, the single-masted Barking smack, used to be a familiar sight on the lower reaches of the Thames, while the Old Granary buildings along Town Quay bear witness to former maritime trade. Eastbury Manor House off Ripple Road (Upney station, District Line) is a late Tudor building which may be viewed by prior arrangement (tel. 081 592 4500, extn. 3241).

Dagenham is reached by joining an eastbound District Line train at Barking, which proceeds by way of Upney and Becontree, where a 1,670-acre estate built between 1921 and 1929 was the largest housing development in Europe. Dagenham Heathway follows, but Dagenham East is arguably more convenient for historic Dagenham village where the fifteenth-century Cross Keys pub is a converted tannery and the 1930s Civic Centre which has an impressive painted ceiling has attained listed building status. The Chase at Eastbrookend is earmarked as a nature reserve and country park, but Chadwell Heath station (page 69) is more convenient for Valence House, a fifteenth-century manor where items of local interest are assembled.

An otherwise monotonous scene is relieved by large open spaces at Mayesbrook Park and Parsloes Park (L) and a brief interlude of scrubland between Dagenham East and Elm Park, watered by the Beam River. RAF Hornchurch was an important part of Britain's wartime air defences, but the aerodrome finally closed in 1962. St Andrew's Church, Hornchurch, with a massive copper-covered tower 120 feet high, possesses a bull's head and horns which have been there for some 400 years, perhaps a reminder of the former tanning industry. There is also a monument to Thomas Witherings, who in 1633 originated the Post Office as we know it today. Between 1926 and 1936, the local population increased sixfold when the London County Council built 16,000 homes in the area.

The Romford branch (page 69) converges (L) at **Upminster**, and a windmill comes into sight (R) as we run into the station. Built in 1803–4, this fine white smock-mill is sometimes open to visitors. Bidding farewell at last to Underground trains, which are stabled at a huge depot (L) beyond Upminster station, the Grays branch (page 69) swings away (R) and crossing open country we come to **West Horndon** station which, curiously, was called East Horndon until 1949. A further stretch of farmland brings us to **Laindon**, the nucleus about which, since 1951, Basildon New Town has grown. Its vast sprawl stretches away on either side, but until **Basildon** station opened in 1974 the nearest rail service was at Laindon. During the 1920s a plotland settlement, now largely vanished, evolved at nearby Dunton; one of the little bungalows has been restored as a museum. At **Pitsea** the line is joined (R) by the Tilbury loop (page 73) and a country park has been named in memory of Wat Tyler who led the Peasants' Revolt.

Distant Kentish oil terminals are visible (R) on the Isle of Grain as the train approaches **Benfleet**, railhead for Canvey Island, named after a Saxon chief who claimed it for his tribe. The land would then have been some twelve feet higher above river level, for over the years the ground sank until in the seventeenth century Canvey was often liable to serious flooding. A Dutch engineer, Cornelius Vermuyden, was commissioned and by 1623 he had built a sea wall around the island. A Canvey farmer teased Daniel Defoe when he made his *Tour Through the Whole Island of Great Britain* (1724–7), telling him that there were no wives to be found on Canvey and that the men had to resort to the Essex uplands to find spouses, who, in the damp climate of pestilence-ridden, fog-shrouded Canvey, died fairly quickly, leaving the poor widower to seek a successor. Defoe evidently believed this, for he wrote of the Canvey

Islander who was living with his twenty-fifth wife whilst having a 35-year-old son who was living with his fourteenth! Canvey has suffered serious inundations, after each of which it was rewalled, most recently in 1953, when fifty-eight islanders died in the floods. Home to 27,000 people, the island has a two-mile horse ride around the base of the sea wall.

From now on the line stays close to, though not always within sight of, the Thames estuary, and as the train proceeds towards Southend the ruins of Hadleigh Castle (English Heritage) are visible on a hillside (L). Built in 1231 and used as a hunting lodge by some kings, and as a river defence by others, it was even given as part of a dowry to various queens, including three of Henry VIII's six wives. Lord Rich bought the site from Edward VI and used it as a quarry; a landslide ensued which demolished a large part of the building, and today very little remains of the most important medieval castle in Essex.

The next station, the first of several within the boundary of Southend, serves **Leigh-on-Sea**; this is something of a misnomer, as it is actually on the river, with the Kentish shore visible (R) on the skyline. Serried ranks of boarding houses (L) salute the train's progress towards **Chalkwell** and on to **Westcliff**, which also likes to think it's 'on-sea'. For visitors who prefer a quiet sojourn, these places offer a peaceful antidote to the brashness and garish lights of Southend itself, which is conveniently served by **Southend Central** station. The famous pier is glimpsed (R) as the train forges on to **Southend East**, where the seaside image gives way to suburbia. Passing **Thorpe Bay** we soon arrive at **Shoeburyness**, a terminus on the outskirts of Southend. This station was originally built to serve an army gunnery school, and sidings still serve ranges beyond Pig's Bay. If you leave the station, cross the road and walk along a grassy area opposite, you will come to the river and a small beach. At this stage, the river estuary is so wide that the Kentish shore is often out of sight. Firing still takes place in the vicinity and notices are posted on the front showing when such activity takes place and the extent of the danger areas.

NORTH KENT: LONDON TO GRAVESEND

by Tim Young

There are four routes between London and Gravesend by rail, or to be more precise between London Bridge and Dartford, where they reunite. This network, collectively known as the North Kent Lines, has a half-hourly off-peak service over each route, giving eight trains each hour to Dartford, of which four go forward to serve Gravesend. On Sundays the service is only slightly less generous. Present rolling stock, amongst the oldest and scruffiest on BR, is soon to be replaced by a fleet of modern trains which it is hoped will improve the lot of the vast army of commuters who use these intensive services.

Our journey starts at **Charing Cross**, just around the corner from one of the capital's most famous sights, Trafalgar Square, with its fountains, the lions sculpted by Landseer, and Nelson atop his 145-foot-high column. Charing Cross is also of significance to road users, since the cross in the station forecourt is the point from which distances to and from London are measured. This cross, erected in 1865, is a Victorian replica of an original Eleanor Cross (page 59) destroyed by Puritans during the Commonwealth. The station occupies the site of Hungerford Market and stands close to a blacking factory where Charles Dickens worked as a boy, and which is mentioned in his novel *David Copperfield*. Train services commenced in 1864 and the following year a 250-bedroom hotel designed by E. M. Barry was opened above the station.

Setting out, the train passes above the Victoria Embankment and then crosses the Thames by Hungerford Bridge, which also accommodates a pedestrian footway. This structure replaced an earlier bridge whose suspension links were salvaged for reuse on Brunel's Clifton Suspension Bridge at Bristol. London's former County Hall is seen ahead (R), looking across the water to the Palace of Westminster, and St Stephen's Tower which houses Big Ben. Contrary to popular belief this is the name of the 13½-ton bell within, not of the clock itself, and recalls the first Commissioner of Works Sir Benjamin Hall, after whom it was named in 1856. As the train reaches the south bank, the Royal Festival Hall is alongside (L) with the Hayward Gallery and Queen Elizabeth Hall beyond, and the magnificent Victory Arch entrance to Waterloo main line terminus (page 13) faces us (R) as the train runs into **Waterloo (East)**, a station unusual in that its four platforms are lettered (A to D) instead of being numbered.

As the train sets off again at rooftop level, the familiar dome of St Paul's Cathedral (page 45) can be glimpsed (L) as a line carrying Thameslink services trails in followed by a triangular junction with lines to Cannon Street. Southwark Cathedral (L), hemmed in by mean streets below Borough Market Junction, is a beautiful restored medieval church at the south end of London Bridge, heart of an Anglican diocese and an important part of the local community, where lunchtime and evening music have become an established feature. In the same vicinity stood Shakespeare's Globe Theatre, and the Rose Theatre whose remains have recently been unearthed. The great bulk of Guy's Hospital (R), founded in 1721 by bookseller Thomas Guy, ushers us into **London Bridge** station, a large complex whose vast glass roof is carried on fifteen miles of steel girders.

In dark echoing vaults beneath, entered from Tooley Street, mystery and surprise lurk around every corner at the London Dungeon, where history's legends and dark secrets are revealed with awesome realism; the contrasting sensations of space travel and the world of Dr Who and his foes can be experienced at 'Space Adventure'. Different chapters of maritime history are represented by the graceful schooner *Kathleen and May*, built in 1900 for coastal trade and preserved at St Mary Overy Dock, Cathedral Street, whilst massive Second World War veteran HMS *Belfast*, Europe's largest preserved warship, lies moored on the river near Morgans Lane. Riverbus services are an unusual way to see the sights, and a service linking Chelsea with Docklands calls at London Bridge City Pier. A short walk along Tooley Street leads to Tower Bridge, one of the most famous sights in the world and seen here to advantage against a backdrop of the ancient Tower of London, redolent with English history. Opened in 1894, Tower Bridge cost over £1 million to build. Twin high-level walkways reached by hydraulic lift were soon closed due to the number of suicide attempts, but now enclosed they once again provide a superb aerial view of London. There is also much more to see when visiting this magnificent feat of Victorian engineering and you may even be fortunate enough to see the huge bascules open for a passing ship: now, alas, a rare occurrence. When this or any other of London's bridges over the Thames is undergoing repair, a bale of hay, easily enough obtained before the advent of motorised transport, is suspended from it as a warning to shipping. An odd custom, it is said to have originated in Roman times. Close to the northern approach, St Katherine's Dock has become a leisure centre where historic vessels lie alongside shops, pubs and restaurants.

Resuming the journey, gaps between buildings (L) reveal views of the Tower of London and Tower Bridge as the train hurries through Bermondsey on a long viaduct built for the London & Greenwich Railway which opened in 1836. It was flanked by

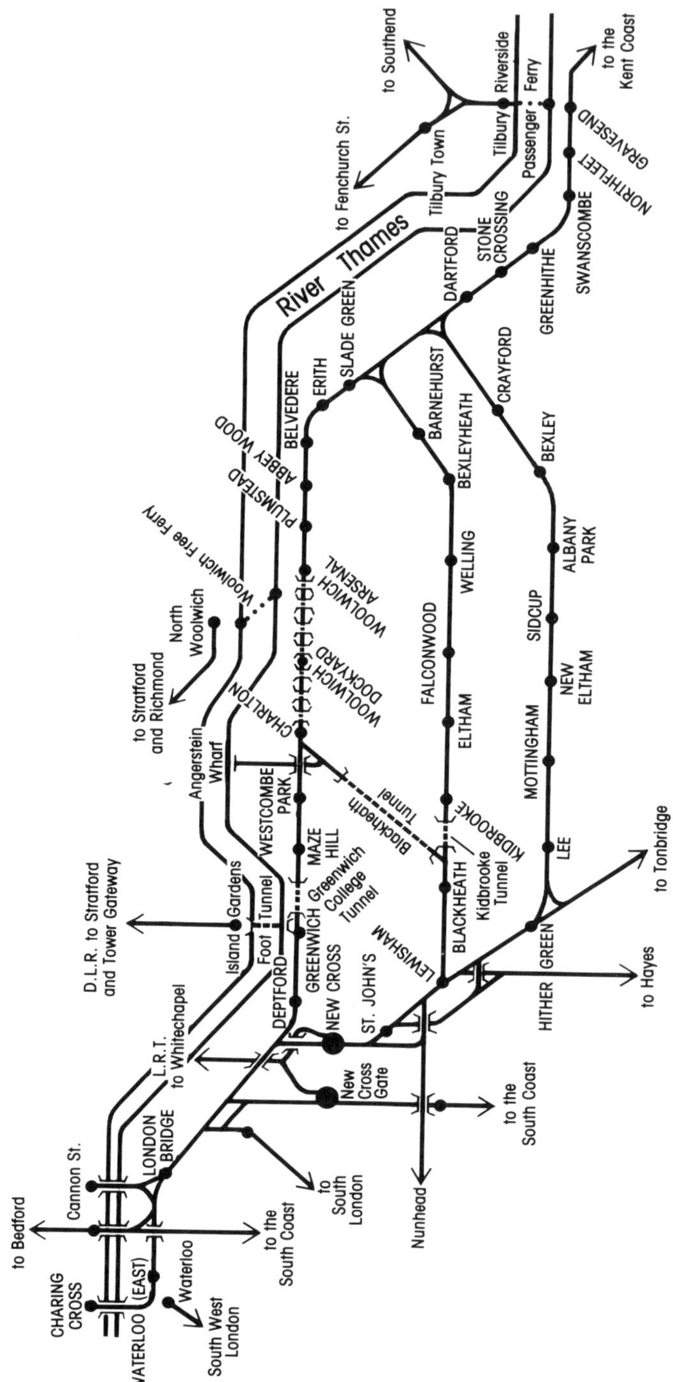

River Thames
to Southend
to Fenchurch St.
Tilbury Town
Tilbury
Riverside
Passenger
Ferry
to the Kent Coast
GRAVESEND
NORTHFLEET
SWANSCOMBE
GREENHITHE
STONE CROSSING
DARTFORD
SLADE GREEN
ERITH
BELVEDERE
ABBEY WOOD
PLUMSTEAD
Woolwich Free Ferry
North Woolwich
to Stratford and Richmond
WOOLWICH ARSENAL
WOOLWICH DOCKYARD
CHARLTON
Angerstein Wharf
WESTCOMBE PARK
MAZE HILL
Blackheath Tunnel
Greenwich College Tunnel
GREENWICH
Island Gardens
Foot Tunnel
D.L.R. to Stratford and Tower Gateway
DEPTFORD
L.R.T. to Whitechapel
NEW CROSS
New Cross Gate
ST. JOHN'S
LEWISHAM
BLACKHEATH
Kidbrooke Tunnel
KIDBROOKE
ELTHAM
FALCONWOOD
WELLING
BEXLEYHEATH
BARNEHURST
CRAYFORD
BEXLEY
ALBANY PARK
SIDCUP
NEW ELTHAM
MOTTINGHAM
LEE
HITHER GREEN
to Tonbridge
to Hayes
to the South Coast
Nunhead
to South London
LONDON BRIDGE
Cannon St.
to Bedford
CHARING CROSS
WATERLOO (EAST)
Waterloo
to South West London
to the South Coast

Tower Bridge, from Butler's Wharf (*Photo:* H. Atkinson)

tree-lined boulevards, for the brick arches were originally intended as homes, but prospective residents were not forthcoming and they were eventually let for commercial use. Features of the original structure repay closer inspection from street level, but from our vantage point little trace is seen of former stations at Spa Road (reminder of a long-vanished chalybeate spring) and Southwark Park. Windswept South Bermondsey station sits airily aloft (R) as lines to Peckham Rye and New Cross Gate peel away, and then the train crosses the East London section of the Metropolitan Line which divides, sending branches to New Cross Gate and New Cross. Floodlight pylons (R) are those of 'The Den', home of Millwall Football Club which moved here from the Isle of Dogs in 1910, and at North Kent East Junction the train parts company with those travelling via Blackheath, Eltham and Sidcup (pages 80–81), bearing left to reach **Deptford**. Across Deptford Creek the tall masts of the clipper *Cutty Sark* welcome us to **Greenwich** (page 67).

Snaking downhill, Greenwich College Tunnel takes trains beneath the National Maritime Museum to resurface at **Maze Hill**, close to both the museum and Greenwich Park. Lineside allotments appear near **Westcombe Park** where the line crosses the southern approach to the Blackwall Tunnel, the oldest road tunnel under the Thames. Built between 1889 and 1897, its roof is in places only five feet below the water (bus 108 for Wanstead, from Westcombe Hill near the station, goes through the tunnel to Stratford). A freight branch to Angerstein Wharf is also encountered before the train joins a route (R) used by trains via Blackheath. We shall consider this route before continuing the journey via Charlton (page 80).

From **New Cross**, where Metropolitan trains terminate alongside (L), these services continue past Tanners Hill Junction near **St John's**, where a line coming in (R) was part of the Greenwich Park branch closed in 1916. **Lewisham**, where lines diverge to the south, sits astride the Greenwich Meridian, whose line is marked in the station subway. Beyond **Blackheath**, home of one of the world's oldest golf clubs (the Royal Blackheath) and the curious oriental Pagoda House, trains routed via Eltham (page 81) branch off (R) before the Blackheath Tunnel which burrows under Shooters Hill. Regaining open air, the Greenwich line is rejoined at Charlton Junction (L) as a branch leaves for Angerstein Wharf. Opened in 1852 by John Angerstein, this branch serves freight terminals on the Thames.

Charlton was the station for 'The Valley', where Charlton Athletic Football Club used to play before deciding, in 1985, to share Selhurst Park with neighbours Crystal Palace. Today, however, it attracts visitors who come for a different reason: to see and marvel at the mighty Thames Barrier. Described as the eighth wonder of the world, it is vital to London's flood defences, for without its protection there is a very real risk that under certain conditions much of the capital would be inundated. A lively and informative visitor centre has been thoughtfully provided to offer an insight into its operation (tel. 081 854 1373). The first mulberry tree in England was planted at Charlton House during the reign of James I in an attempt to introduce silkworm cultivation. St Luke's Church was a landmark for shipping, and from its tower was flown the Red Ensign, rather than the flag of St George.

During the following two miles, a series of tunnels and deep cuttings take the line through Woolwich where the next station, **Woolwich Dockyard**, is a reminder of long-established links with the armed services. The Royal Dockyard closed in 1869 and became a War Department store, but the Woolwich Free Ferry, opened in 1889, still plies across the Thames to North Woolwich and the North London Line (page 29). However, it is chiefly with the army that one associates Woolwich, traditional home of the Royal School of Artillery. The frontage of the impressive RA Barracks extends over 1,000 feet and stands on the edge of Woolwich Common, which until the late nineteenth-century was used for live firing practice, which occasionally, and perhaps not surprisingly, caused injury to both people and property. A regimental museum containing a wide variety of arms from many periods is housed at the Rotunda, a circular building designed by John Nash as a tent for the allied sovereigns' meeting of 1814 at St James's Park. Five years later it was moved to this site and an outer shell added. Buildings of the adjacent Royal Military Academy, founded in 1741 and merged in 1946 with the Royal Military College, Sandhurst, were erected in 1806 to a design by Sir Jeffry Wyatville.

Woolwich Arsenal station is adjacent to the former Royal Arsenal, first established in 1716, which eventually covered some 1,200 acres, gave its name to a Cooperative Society and spawned a First Division football club. In its early days Arsenal did not aspire to glory, success only following a move to Highbury in 1913 and its promotion to League Division One in 1919. **Plumstead**, a former fishing village, was also famed for its apple orchards, long since covered by dense housing. Its most famous son of recent years is snooker player Steve Davis. On the common, a disused windmill has been incorporated in the Old Mill pub. Woolwich Arsenal was served by over 120 miles of railway, which diverged (L) just after Plumstead station, and even operated its own internal passenger service. After 1919, part of the factory was for a time devoted to locomotive building. The complex was run down during the 1960s and 1970s and the area now forms part of the developing Thamesmead district (L), served also by a station at **Abbey Wood**. Adjacent wooded parkland shelters the fragmentary remains of Lesnes Abbey, a small Augustinian community founded in 1178 by Richard de Lucy of Ongar Castle (page 108).

Belvedere is on the edge of Plumstead Marshes (L), once a firing range but now harbouring light industry, and site of a remarkable Victorian pumping station at the

Southern Outfall works, Crossness. **Erith** hogs the riverside and at **Slade Green** there is a triangular junction (R), opposite carriage sheds, with a line from Lewisham via Welling. The description of the journey to Gravesend resumes below.

Passengers on the Welling route branch off (R) after Blackheath, entering a tunnel which extends to **Kidbrooke**, named after a local stream. **Eltham**, opened in 1986, replaced stations at Eltham (Well Hall) and Eltham Park, when the track was re-aligned to accommodate a new road (R). A vanished eighteenth-century house at Well Hall Pleasaunce (L) had literary connections; a moat, walls and barn survive from an earlier Tudor house. Eltham Palace, about three-quarters of a mile away, was a royal residence until it was largely destroyed by Cromwellian troops. It was later rebuilt and became the headquarters of the Institute of Army Education, but parts of the earlier building remain, including the late fifteenth-century Great Hall with its splendid hammer-beam roof (English Heritage). **Falconwood** is reached after crossing Eltham Park's green acres, followed by stations at **Welling** and **Bexleyheath** before the line passes from London into Kent near **Barnehurst**. Alight at Welling and take bus 51 (bound for Orpington) to Blackfen Road where the Jolly Farmer pub brews beer on the premises, a process which visitors can see for themselves (tel. 081 850 6664). Landscaped Danson Park surrounds an eighteenth-century mansion, and the thirteenth-century former parish church of St Michael has become a Greek Orthodox church. After Barnehurst, a spur used by a few rush-hour trains departs (L) for Slade Green before the train joins the main line from Greenwich (L) at Crayford Creek Junction. Bridging the River Cray, a triangular junction (R) with a line via Sidcup (below) brings the train to Dartford. The description of the journey from here to Gravesend resumes below.

Trains travelling by the Sidcup route head south from **Lewisham** and negotiating the Courthill Loop leave the so-called Mid-Kent Line (L), crossing the diminutive Ravensbourne to reach **Hither Green**. Kent Coast trains sweep away (R), throwing off a curve which comes in (R) near **Lee**, in the heartland of semi-detached suburbia, where **Mottingham** station is also convenient for visiting Eltham Palace. **New Eltham** and **Sidcup** serve a populous hinterland laid out with spacious parkland, and **Albany Park** opened in 1935 to serve new housing. **Bexley** has a much restored church, St Mary the Virgin, with an unusual octagonal shingled spire, and Hall Place is a historic mansion standing in beautiful gardens beside the River Cray. Former Prime Minister Edward Heath represents the local parliamentary constituency of Old Bexley. The silk-printing works of David Evans & Company at Bourne Road, **Crayford**, are open to visitors by appointment (tel. 081 0322 57576) and there is also a mill shop. Further information about the area is available from the London Borough of Bexley (tel. 081 858 6376). After the train crosses the M2, a triangular junction (whose western side is not used by passenger trains) unites us with trains from the other routes near **Dartford**.

This is the start of the Darent Valley Path, a waymarked riverside walk of about six miles which crosses attractive country southwards to Farningham, where walkers can either join a train at Farningham Road station or continue to the pleasant village of Eynsford, which also has a station.

Burrough's Wellcome Pharmaceutical works can be seen (L), and Dartford used also to be the home of J. E. Hall, makers of escalators, whose deserted works stand forlornly boarded up. As the train emerges from a cutting, the distant skyline is punctuated by a brightly coloured flume tower at 'Fantasias' water complex, which caters for all ages and abilities in a simulated tropical atmosphere. Still under construction, the new Dartford Bridge rears skywards (L), its deck rising in an arc high above the river to accommodate shipping. Passengers boarding at **Stone Crossing** purchase tickets from the crossing keeper's hut alongside Cutton Lane. The massive chimneys of Purfleet Cement Works are visible (L) on the Essex shore as trains approach **Greenhithe**. Extensive workings beyond **Swanscombe** are evidence of cement manufacture on the Kentish shore at **Northfleet**. Cement is basically a mixture of chalk, clay and gypsum, which is then fused together in a furnace. With chalk and clay readily available locally, and gypsum shipped in by river, it is easy to understand why cement manufacture is a major industry here.

Continuing the journey, a long straight embankment (R) carried a branch line from Farningham Road to Gravesend West which closed to passengers in 1953. At **Gravesend** the station, which once bore the apt suffix 'Central', is in the middle of town. One can either explore, or take the Sealink ferry for a five-minute crossing to Tilbury and a different route back to London (page 73). The ferry landing is about ten minutes' walk from the station. The ferry's value will, however, be seriously diminished should Tilbury Riverside station (page 73) close. Journeys beyond Gravesend are described in *Kent and East Sussex by Rail*.

GRAVESEND

by Tim Young

Any account of Gravesend must inevitably involve three people: General Gordon, Charles Dickens and, unlikeliest of all, Pocahontas, a Red Indian princess.

On 21 March 1617 a small rowing boat set off from a ship, *The George*, moored in the Thames off Gravesend, and headed for the Kentish shore. On board was the body of a young woman of twenty-two who was carried to a nearby churchyard and buried quietly, without fuss or ceremony. In 1608, at the age of thirteen, she had saved the life of Captain John Smith, leader of the first settlement in the British colony of Chesapeake, Virginia. He had been captured by Red Indians and sentenced to death, but as the executioner prepared to end his life, Pocahontas threw herself across him after vainly pleading with her father, the tribal chief, to spare the prisoner's life. The story of how this brave girl had saved his life was later recounted by John Smith in a letter to Queen Anne, wife of King James I. Pocahontas later became a Christian, taking the name Rebecca. In 1613 she met another settler, John Rolfe, the colony's secretary and recorder, and they were married the following year. Her husband brought her to England and Pocahontas, now Mrs Rebecca Rolfe, was presented at Court. Everyone was impressed by her gentleness and charm, but in an alien climate she became ill and the Rolfes resolved to return to America. Sadly, Pocahontas died before their ship set sail and she was laid to rest in an unmarked grave, the first American to be buried on British shores. However, her last resting place is thought to be somewhere in the precincts of the present St George's Church, which replaced an earlier building destroyed by fire in 1727. Accordingly, it has become a place of pilgrimage for visiting Americans and the churchyard, now free of headstones and renamed Pocahontas Gardens, has a bronze statue of the princess, presented by her countrymen.

Dickensian associations with the area are numerous, although there are no relevant sites in the town centre. Dickens and his wife spent their honeymoon in 1836 at Chalk, a village on the way to Rochester. Their landlady, a Mrs Craddock, was later immortalised in *The Pickwick Papers*, and the local smithy was most likely Joe Gargery's forge in *Great Expectations*. On the canal bank at Gravesend is a house formed from an upturned boat, similar to Mr Peggotty's in *David Copperfield*, and in the same novel Messrs Peggotty, Ham and Micawber emigrated to Australia from Gravesend. The Ship and Lobster at Denton, an eastern suburb, was probably the

Ship in *Great Expectations*, which is set on the marshes around Gravesend, but the best-known link is Gads Hill Place at Higham (served by the next station towards Rochester). Now a girls' school, it was Dickens' home from 1856 until his death in 1870, and buildings in the village featured in some of his novels.

Charles Gordon was posted to Gravesend in 1865 at the age of twenty-two to build forts for defending the Thames. He lived at Fort House and allowed local folk to stroll in the gardens on summer evenings. He taught regularly at the 'Ragged School' and, a committed Christian, he was an ardent evangelist. In 1884 General Gordon was appointed Governor General of the Sudan and the following year he was murdered at the Siege of Khartoum. Fort House was destroyed in 1944, but the gardens remain open to the public and feature a terracotta statue of Gordon. Also in the gardens are Milton Chantry (English Heritage), a chapel dating from 1322, and the New Tavern Fort, built in the 1780s and remodelled by Gordon in 1870. Gordon Promenade, a grassed area, looks across the water to Tilbury, and breezy Windmill Hill, reached by footpath from Clarence Place, affords spectacular views of the town and river from its summit. Three stones mark the places where bombs fell on the hill in the First World War. At Rosherville the last of the old pleasure gardens in the style of fashionable Vauxhall and Ranelagh closed about eighty years ago.

Back in town, an impressive white clock tower was raised by public subscription in 1887 to celebrate Queen Victoria's Golden Jubilee, and it used to be the terminus of a lengthy stage service to Brighton. Near the ferry terminal, the Town Pier of 1834 is a grade II listed building whose timber superstructure has classical embellishments.

JOINTLY TO AYLESBURY

by Ian McGill

Marylebone is a modest terminus at the rump end of the erstwhile Great Central Railway, whose London Extension line from Nottingham, opened in 1899, represented the swan song of nineteenth-century railway building. Undergoing a period of strained relations with the Metropolitan Railway, over which its trains approached the capital, the GCR sought alternative access; coincidentally the Great Western Railway, under pressure of competition from the rival London & North Western Railway, was seeking to provide quicker journeys to Birmingham than were possible via Oxford. Both companies found a common solution to their problems by creating a new route, based partly on existing lines, which would achieve their separate aims. Opened in the early years of this century, the former Great Western & Great Central Joint Railway forms the basis of this journey.

In decline for many years, it was inevitable that Marylebone's future as a railway terminus would eventually come under scrutiny, and thus in 1983 closure was proposed. Allied to an extension of Metropolitan Line trains to Aylesbury and diversion of remaining services via Princes Risborough to serve Paddington, there might have been some positive benefits, but vigorous opposition prompted a rethink, and the station is to be retained, new signalling installed and a fleet of modern trains introduced as part of a revitalised Chiltern Lines network.

There are two routes to Aylesbury. Trains via Amersham, with which we are not really concerned here, run at half-hourly intervals Mondays to Fridays and hourly at weekends, but on Sundays one must travel from Baker Street (LRT) and change at Amersham (page 96). The scenically superior route is via Princes Risborough (weekdays only), and trains operate at two-hourly intervals, normally carrying the

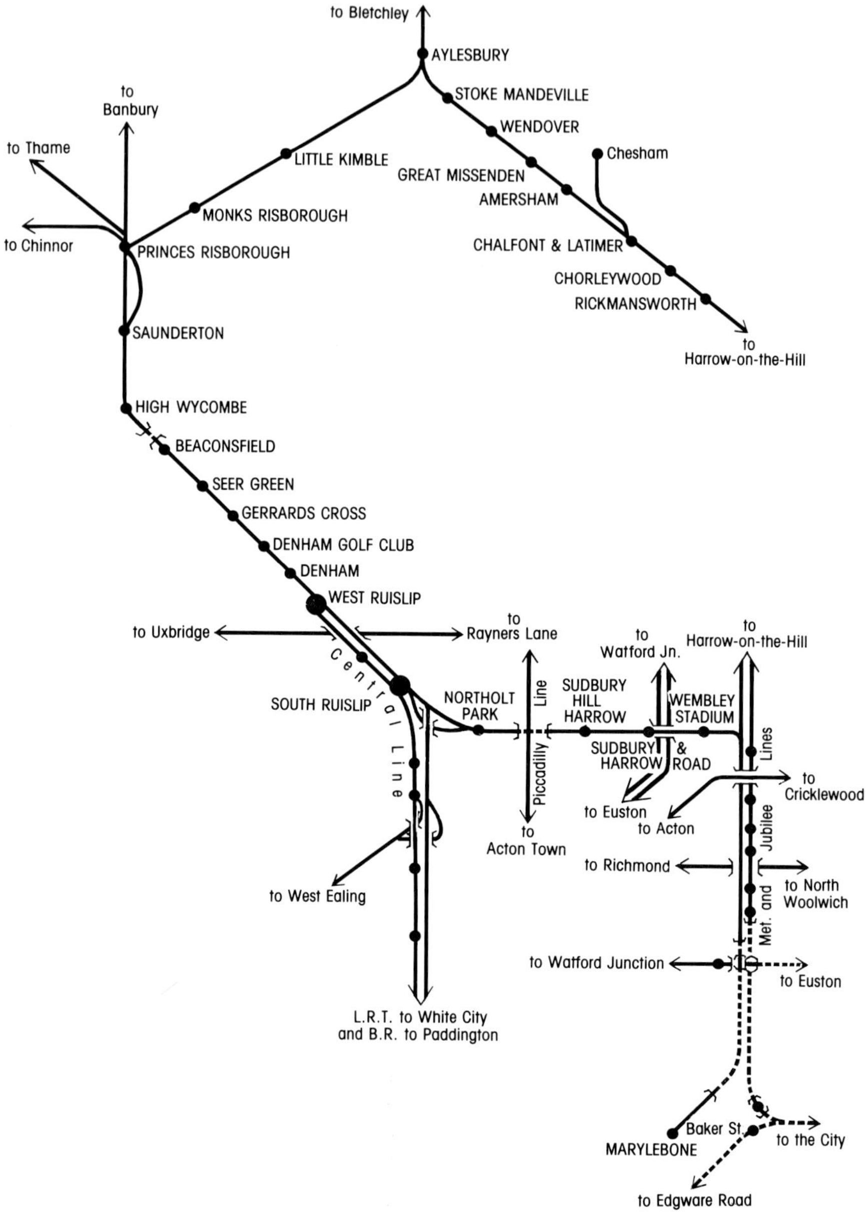

destination display 'Little Kimble' in order to avoid confusion with the direct train to Aylesbury which departs a few minutes earlier. The journey takes about eighty-five minutes. Between London and Princes Risborough the service is supplemented by two-hourly trains which continue to Banbury (see *Thames and Downs by Rail*). It should, however, be noted that Sudbury & Harrow Road, Sudbury Hill (Harrow) and South Ruislip stations have only limited Monday to Friday services.

Blocks of flats (L) occupy the former **Marylebone** goods depot site, and the Grand Union Canal is bridged adjacent to the Metropolitan Line (R), before trains plunge into a series of tunnels expensively constructed beneath palatial St John's Wood and the hallowed ground of Lord's, a name revered among cricket lovers all over the world. Headquarters and birthplace of the Marylebone Cricket Club (MCC) which was founded about 1787, Lord's is also home to Middlesex County Cricket Club. The present ground was acquired for the MCC by their groundsman Thomas Lord after whom it is named. Ironically, this jealously guarded shrine was almost lost to cricket when Lord, aware of its worth for building, later attempted to dispose of the site. Despite the railway tunnels, property demolition was inevitable, and bricks salvaged as a result were reused in retaining walls on this part of the railway works. At the second of two breaks in the tunnel, the train passes above South Hampstead station (L) and the lines from Euston, finally emerging from the gloomy underworld behind Finchley Road Underground station (R). For the next 2½ miles it runs parallel with LRT trains to reach Neasden South Junction. While passengers for Aylesbury via Harrow continue along the original GCR route in company with Metropolitan and Jubilee Line trains, services via High Wycombe branch off here, to reach **Wembley Stadium** station.

Perhaps best known as the annual venue for the FA Cup Final, Wembley Stadium was built for the 1924 British Empire Exhibition, but had actually opened a few months earlier to stage the 1923 FA Challenge Cup Final. Later it hosted many events of the 1948 Olympic Games which were held in London, and to facilitate better access to Wembley Park station (page 92), Olympic Way was driven across the old exhibition site, which provided turf for the original Wembley pitch. Guided tours are available on most days when major events are not in progress (tel. 081 903 4864). Wembley Arena (built in 1924 as the Empire Pool) and Conference Centre stand nearby and a few of the palaces and pavilions built for the 1924 exhibition survive in varying degrees of decrepitude, mostly converted for industrial or warehousing purposes and largely hidden among more recent developments.

Deep cuttings colonised by birch and rowan trees are held back by stout retaining walls constructed of blue engineering brick and, characteristic of a bold approach to civil engineering at the turn of the century, testify to the late arrival of this line. Harrow-on-the-Hill (page 98) can be seen above the rooftops (R) and there is a second encounter with the lines out of Euston which are crossed shortly before Barham Park appears as a green oasis (L) among spacious suburban homes. Owned by Sir George Barham, chairman of the Express Dairy Company, which maintained a model dairy in the park, the estate passed on his death to the local authority for use as a public open space. Adjacent **Sudbury & Harrow Road** station is quite close to Sudbury Town LRT station, and for the next mile or so both BR and Piccadilly Line Underground trains keep close company, albeit out of sight of one another. **Sudbury Hill (Harrow)** is but a few yards from Sudbury Hill Underground station, but is more than a mile south of Harrow, for which it is not a recommended railhead unless you are prepared to tackle the intervening distance on foot. A short tunnel through a spur of Harrow Hill also takes BR trains beneath the Underground as the Piccadilly Line, tiring of its sport with an alien railway, sweeps northwards to seek a lasting relationship with its own kind at Rayners Lane (page 93).

Northolt Park station was not contemporary with its neighbours, having been opened in 1929 alongside a newly established racecourse. In 1938 a race meeting at Northolt Park was one of BBC Television's first outside broadcasts of a sporting event, but the moment of glory was brief for the course was comandeered for military purposes in 1939 and with a return to peace was eventually given over to housing. The north-western suburbs slobber hungrily in a frenzy of nondescript rooftops around distant wooded heights (R) beyond Ruislip. 'Up' and 'down' lines diverge, climbing independently to meet a little-used route from Paddington which once carried GWR Birmingham expresses, and then runs in tandem with Central Line Underground trains (L) which provide the main service at **South Ruislip**, where few BR trains call. A refuse transfer station, established here by the former Greater London Council, despatches trainloads of containerised rubbish to landfill sites in Buckinghamshire. As the train traverses a mainly residential district, the hangars of Northolt Aerodrome, an RAF station which played an important part in the Battle of Britain, are prominent (L). Later used for some civilian flights, the airfield has since reverted to a purely military role. Beyond Ruislip Gardens Central Line station (L) a network of tracks serves LRT's huge West Ruislip depot, which is connected with BR in order to facilitate delivery and dispersal of stock.

The Metropolitan's Uxbridge branch (page 93) passes below near **West Ruislip** station, where Central Line trains terminate on the fringe of suburbia. It was proposed at one time to project them westwards to Denham, but very little was done towards pursuing this plan, although token evidence remains in the form of a wide embankment (L). South Harefield Halt, closed in 1931, had been optimistically provided where a cutting opens out into the Colne Valley, in anticipation of building work which failed to materialise. A short branch, with an equally short career, trailed in (L) from Uxbridge, and rumbling across the Grand Union Canal and River Colne, trains pass into Buckinghamshire near **Denham**, where producer Alexander Korda established his film studios – Britain's Hollywood – north of the line. Alas, the great days of the silver screen have passed, and with them Denham Studios, which are being redeveloped for industrial use. Attractive Denham village, set amid warm undulating Home Counties countryside, is just south of its station. **Denham Golf Club** basks among birches overlooking the Misbourne, and besides golfers also used to cater for flying club patrons at Denham Airfield.

The busy M25 and A413 are encountered on the way to **Gerrards Cross** where a new platform is being provided (R) on a site originally occupied by the old through lines. Chalfont St Peter, about a mile north of the station, is now virtually united to Gerrards Cross. Gott's Monument was erected in 1785 by Sir Henry Gott of nearby Newlands Park, supposedly to mark the spot where King George III slew a stag. However, it eventually served a more useful purpose as a milestone, giving distances to London, Denham and Uxbridge. Newlands Park has become the Chiltern Open Air Museum where redundant buildings of historic significance otherwise doomed to demolition have been painstakingly re-erected. The more appealing village of Chalfont St Giles (to which Seer Green station is closer) lies a little further afield. Both villages are named from the dedication of their churches, but it was to peaceful Chalfont St Giles that the poet John Milton came in 1665 to escape the Great Plague. Embittered by loneliness and handicapped by blindness, it was here that the aging Milton wrote *Paradise Lost*, a work which earned him five pounds! Later, consoled by a Quaker friend and having come to terms with misfortune, he was to pen the sequel, *Paradise Regained*. The cottage where Milton lived still stands and is open to visitors. Bertram Mills, of circus fame, lies buried in the village churchyard. Behind a mansion known as The Vache stands a monument to Captain James Cook (1728–79), explorer and navigator.

A series of deep cuttings and lofty embankments convey trains boldly onwards through the Chilterns to **Seer Green** (formerly Seer Green & Jordans). Set in fine woodland scenery away from main roads, Jordans is known for its associations with William Penn. A member of the Society of Friends (Quakers), he was frequently imprisoned for his beliefs before emigrating to America, where he founded the State of Pennsylvania. A burial ground, where the simple headstones include one marking William Penn's grave, was purchased by the Friends in 1671, but the little plain brick Meeting House was not erected until 1688, immediately after King James II issued the

Declaration of Indulgence which recognised the rights of dissenters. Old Jordans Farm, where Quakers met previously, later became a youth hostel, and nearby stands the Mayflower Barn, reputedly built from the timbers of a ship, some of which may have originated from the *Mayflower*, on which the Pilgrim Fathers set sail in 1620 for freedom in the New World.

Before long the outlying houses of **Beaconsfield** peer hesitantly over a rise and as rapidly disappear, obscured by a cutting which brings us to the station. There are some elegant houses and coaching inns in the older part of Beaconsfield, including the Royal White Hart where Queen Elizabeth I stayed, and where Cromwell billeted his troops. The modern town dates from about 1909 and in Warwick Road, a short distance from the station, is Bekonscot, the world's oldest model village, which last year celebrated its sixtieth anniversary. Covering 1½ acres of garden it began as a hobby and now attracts visitors from far and wide who come to see and marvel at the buildings and extensive gauge '1' railway.

Wooburn Moor spreads lethargically across the hillside (L) and then White House Tunnel brings the train into the Wycombe Valley where a branch, closed in 1970, came in (L) from Bourne End. There are extensive views as the train drifts down towards the station, where over-enthusiastic use of an unpleasant shade of green paint gives an unnecessarily drab appearance. **High Wycombe** is a large cosmopolitan town stretching for several untidy miles along the valley; it is an important shopping and commercial centre for a wide surrounding district. Lace-making and straw-plaiting have been important to the town's economy, but High Wycombe is mostly associated with furniture production. A museum contains beautiful examples of local craftsmanship, the inheritance of an age-old tradition of Chiltern bodgers, craftsmen who lived and worked alone in the beech woods. Surviving older buildings include the Guildhall and octagonal Shambles (or Little Market House) in the Market Place, which are especially pleasing. Just north of the town in a lovely parkland setting and sheltered by woods is Hughenden Manor (National Trust), where former Prime Minister Benjamin Disraeli lived. His father Isaac d'Israeli (1766–1848) was a well-known literary figure and indefatigable collector of books. A red granite pillar dating from 1863, at the edge of Great Tinkers Wood, perpetuates his memory.

High Wycombe eventually gives way to a magnificent view (L) of West Wycombe Church, its tower crowned by a distinctive golden ball, and the nearby Dashwood Mausoleum, as the train enters an area of superb scenery. Below, set against a background of wooded slopes, is West Wycombe House, an eighteenth-century mansion in landscaped parkland and home of the Dashwood family. An earlier Sir Francis Dashwood founded the Hell Fire Club, whose mysterious ritualistic activities took place in adjacent caves and for whose members the mausoleum was fashioned, using flint and Portland stone. West Wycombe House and the picturesque village belong to the National Trust; the church, mausoleum and caves do not, but visitors are permitted at certain times. For detailed information please telephone West Wycombe Park office (0494 24411/2). West Wycombe station was an early casualty, having closed in 1958, but bus services are available from High Wycombe (tel. Buckinghamshire County Council enquiry line, see page 111).

With the A4010 tagging along for company past Bradenham (R), the train comes to **Saunderton**, remote from the village it purports to serve, its *raison d'être* an adjacent factory which occupies an enviable situation. Lacey Green crowns a ridge (R), where observant travellers may see the tips of a windmill's sails peering above the trees. Of wooden construction, this is Lacey Green smock-mill, which is considered the oldest windmill of its type in Britain. Opening is usually restricted to summer Sunday afternoons, but, standing in a field behind The Whip public house, it is easily seen from the roadside. There are bus services from Princes Risborough and High Wycombe. The 'up' line dips away (R) into a cutting and through a short tunnel, this

Parish Church of St Mary, Princes Risborough (*Photo:* I. McGill)

separate alignment having been adopted to benefit London-bound expresses. Passing Saunderton (L), some two miles later the lines reunite near **Princes Risborough**, a charming town with time-mellowed buildings, including a fine Georgian Manor House (National Trust) and an arcaded market house of warm-hued brick and tile. The manor once belonged to Edward, Prince of Wales (the Black Prince), eldest son of King Edward III. Only the 'up' side of the station (a mere shadow of its former self) remains in use. Branches to Watlington and Oxford, now truncated goods lines to Chinnor and Thame, disappear behind the signal-box (L), whilst Banbury trains continue straight ahead along a main line which has been reduced to single track; further retrenchment recently took place when the last train tripped a final load of coal down to Chinnor cement works, leaving behind two miles of rusty weed-covered rails, perhaps to be reawakened at some future date as a preservation venture.

In contrast the single-track branch to Aylesbury has, after several years in the doldrums, seen a restoration of regular weekday passenger services. The train curves sharply away, skirting the north side of the town, with St Mary's Church spire prominent among trees (R), the scene dominated by a huge white cross cut into the chalk hillside beyond. Sadly in need of cleaning, this is the Whiteleaf Cross which in its present form probably dates from about the seventeenth century. After about a mile the train pauses alongside Crowbrook Road (R) at **Monks Risborough**, once ecclesiastical property and now virtually one with its larger neighbour. The present platform recently replaced a ramshackle wooden affair known as Monks Risborough & Whiteleaf Halt, which stood on a slightly different site. From here one may make a steep but attractive ascent to the hanging woods above Whiteleaf, allowing time to see the sixteenth-century dovecote near St Dunstan's Church, at the centre of an older Monks Risborough.

Continuing along the foot of the beautiful Chiltern scarp (R), which gently subsides into soft green pasture stretching endlessly away (L) into the fertile Vale of Aylesbury, the train comes to **Little Kimble**, its station building long since converted to a private residence. Little Kimble and its neighbour Great Kimble are diminutive villages, each with an interesting church, and are close to the station. Ellesborough, about a mile distant on the Wendover road, has a magnificent church which presides over a scattered village of thatched cottages and farms under the benign guardianship of ancient hilltop earthworks known as Cymbeline's Castle. Chequers Court, a large mansion presented to the nation by Lord Lee in 1916 for use in perpetuity as a country retreat by serving prime ministers, stands nearby in a secluded setting. The Chilterns' highest viewpoint at Coombe Hill (R) lies towards Wendover, its summit crowned by an obelisk commemorating local men who were killed in South Africa during the Boer War.

The train heads north, across rich meadowland liberally dotted with farms, on the final stage of its journey. After a level-crossing with a minor road, the urban fringes of Aylesbury begin to assert themselves as the tall chimney of Stoke Mandeville Hospital rears skyward (R) and outlying estates close in. Where Mandeville Road draws alongside (R), there is nothing left to mark the site of South Aylesbury Halt, closed in 1967, which was the nearest station to the hospital and marked the boundary of urban development. In a few moments the train driver surrenders a token, his authority to travel over the single line from Princes Risborough, to an **Aylesbury** signalman and thus the journey ends.

It is interesting to reflect at this point that Aylesbury station was unique in being jointly owned by two joint committees of which one partner, the GCR, was common to both. This journey has been over one of those joint routes; most surviving portions of the other – the Metropolitan & Great Central Joint Line – feature in the next chapter, which also includes some material about Aylesbury.

BY UNDERGROUND TO THE COUNTRY I: FROM THE CITY TO METRO-LAND (METROPOLITAN LINE)

by Ian McGill and Peter G. Scott

Conceived as a brilliant marketing ploy by the old Metropolitan Railway for its ventures into Hertfordshire, Buckinghamshire and Middlesex, and later immortalised by the late John Betjeman, 'Metro-land' came to represent much more than a mere advertising gimmick – perhaps even an ideal, a romantic notion of utopian bliss, as sought after, yet as elusive, as the Holy Grail. Join that quest, if you will, on today's Metropolitan Line, whose service of fast and stopping trains makes it a unique part of the Underground and which by virtue of its history has a special status. This is at once evident when boarding a train furnished with high-backed seating and vestigial luggage racks which may suggest, even to travellers unacquainted with the niceties of railway practice, something more than just another Underground railway.

When 'the Met' opened on 10 January 1863 from Paddington to Farringdon, it was the first underground railway in the world, and from this modest beginning expanded to become a major part of the capital's transport system. Cherishing greater ambitions, however, the Met broke free of its urban bondage to send an 'extension line' north-westward, reaching, from 1868 to 1899, distant outposts far from the grimy soot-stained tunnels beneath Bayswater and Clerkenwell. The Met's headquarters were at Baker Street and under the single-minded leadership of its chairman, Sir Edward Watkin, it was fiercely independent, coming to regard itself as a main line

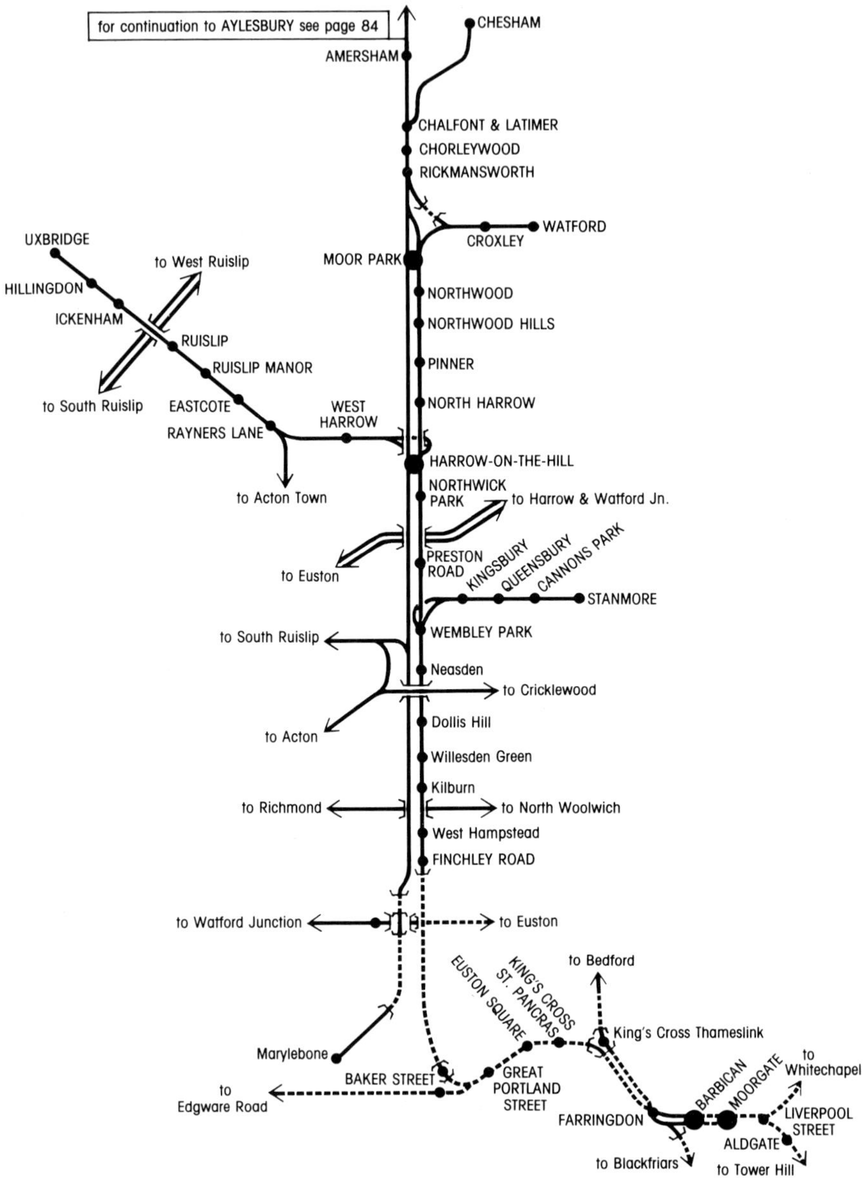

railway with visions of becoming part of a trunk route between Manchester and Paris via a proposed Channel tunnel, but such grandiose aspirations were finally laid to rest in 1933 when it was absorbed into London Transport. Steam trains had by now been banished to the outer regions beyond Rickmansworth, electric locomotives hauling trains of 'slam door' coaches thus far from London. Metropolitan trains, long since curtailed beyond Aylesbury, were further cut back to Amersham and Chesham in 1961 following electrification work completed the previous year.

During weekday rush-hours, some trains start from cramped **Aldgate** station, economically squeezed into the eastern side of the Circle Line and not far from Middlesex Street, where each Sunday at colourful Petticoat Lane Market, Cockney salesmanship may be seen at its best. **Liverpool Street**'s platform 3 (L), closed at the time of writing, was used by some Great Western Railway trains from Hammersmith and Paddington until these ceased in 1939. **Moorgate**, with ten platforms, is among the largest London Regional Transport stations. The bay platforms (L) are used by Metropolitan and Thameslink trains during peak times, whilst BR's Great Northern Suburban services (page 55) depart from low-level platforms, latterly part of the Northern Line but originally an isolated branch of the 'Met'. There is more than shopping and business interest at **Barbican**, where plays by Shakespeare and other dramatists are presented at the Barbican Centre, and opposite the station a new exhibition, Royal Britain, tells the colourful story of Britain's monarchs. Also well worth visiting are the Museum of London and the National Postal Museum. The latter is housed at the Post Office's King Edward Building, which also preserves fragments of the old city walls. Remains of these can also be found at several other places, including the Tower of London, in Jewry Street, at Aldgate, and along a thoroughfare known as London Wall. The adjacent churchyard of St Botolph-without-Aldersgate is known as Postman's Park, where a series of ceramic tablets record acts of heroism by ordinary folk, and which cost them their lives.

After the line tunnels beneath Smithfield Market, where the GWR had an underground goods depot, a brief interval of daylight flooding in among the soaring buildings reveals a glimpse (L) of the curve used by Thameslink services from south London. **Farringdon** station retains an overall roof, giving shelter also to BR trains which call alongside (L) before diving under our path to run parallel (R) through Clerkenwell Tunnels, below an area which has spawned several revolutionaries. The district takes its name from Clerk's Well, a source of water in medieval times, although the water was devoid of any beneficial minerals, unlike its neighbours Bagnigge Wells and London Spa. A disused platform (L) is the site of an earlier King's Cross station, part of which survives behind a wall (R) as King's Cross Thameslink, where trains enter a continuous tunnel beneath Euston Road. The present sub-surface station at **King's Cross St Pancras** opened in 1941, having been re-sited to provide improved interchange with other Underground lines and the main line termini. **Euston Square** station, a few minutes' walk from Euston main line terminus, has no surface buildings, but **Great Portland Street**, unremarkable at platform level, has pleasing well proportioned surface buildings.

Through trains from the City to Finchley Road and beyond branch off (R) in advance of **Baker Street**, station for Madame Tussaud's justly famous waxworks exhibition, and the adjoining London Planetarium which unravels the mysteries of the heavens in a mixture of entertainment and education. A combined admission ticket is available, representing a worthwhile saving. A stroll through tree-shaded Regent's Park brings one to the oldest and most famous zoo in the world, the Royal Zoological Society's London Zoo, which houses over 8,000 animals. Conan Doyle's fictional detective Sherlock Holmes will always be synonymous with this area although neither the character nor his address at 221B Baker Street ever existed in reality. The decor of Baker Street's Jubilee Line platforms fittingly incorporates a Holmes motif in its design, and the memory of his arch-enemy Moriarty is perpetuated in the name of the station bar. The celebrated eighteenth-century actress Sarah Siddons, whose most famous role was that of Lady Macbeth, lived nearby in a house which was eventually engulfed by the railway, but if rumour is to be believed her restless spirit is reluctant to leave.

Impressively dominated by the Edwardian bulk of Chiltern Court above, the Met station still manages, like a gracefully aging maiden aunt, to exude an aura of modest, genteel dignity, echoing those halcyon days when one could travel in Pullman comfort from its canyon-like depths, until the outbreak of war in 1939 hastened the end of such luxury. Today, swift electric trains depart daily at intervals of 15–20 minutes for Watford and Uxbridge, supplemented by half-hourly fast trains for Amersham (connecting at Chalfont for Chesham). In addition, Harrow-on-the-Hill and stations from Moor Park to Amersham (inclusive) are served by British Rail trains which run from Marylebone to Aylesbury (see page 83, also *Thames and Downs by Rail*).

Plunging at once into a tunnel which is briefly punctuated by an encounter with the Grand Union Canal, and by abandoned stations at St John's Wood, Lords and Swiss Cottage, trains emerge at **Finchley Road** for cross-platform connections with Jubilee Line services, and are soon joined by non-electrified BR lines (L) from Marylebone (page 83), which run alongside as far as Harrow-on-the-Hill before surrendering their separate identity. Wembley Park is normally the next stop for Metropolitan trains, quickly reached after passing a succession of Jubilee Line stations serving the inner suburbs. Between West Hampstead and Kilburn the North London Line (page 29) may be seen below, threading its way between the gardens of tall Victorian villas, and a goods line from Cricklewood to Acton wends its way across our path near Neasden, where the large Metropolitan and Jubilee Line depot (R) also maintained a small fleet of active steam locomotives until 1971. This apparent anomaly was due to the fact that they were found to be more economical for some works trains than other forms of motive power.

Large crowds regularly pass through **Wembley Park** station when there are major events at Wembley Stadium (page 85), which marks the site of what came to be known as Watkins' Folly, an immense tower which, had it ever been completed, would have reached a height of 1150 feet, making it taller than the Eiffel Tower in Paris. Commenced largely on the initiative of the Met's chairman, both money and enthusiasm eventually ran out and the rusting monster was finally demolished in 1907. The description of the journey to Harrow and beyond resumes on page 93.

Burrowing junctions carry trains away (R) from Wembley Park to Stanmore. Opened in 1932, this branch, which was later taken over by Bakerloo services and has more recently been appropriated by the Jubilee Line, was the Met's last essay into prospective suburbia. Tapping an area of unspoilt country, new estates rapidly engulfed all but the open spaces at Fryent and Barn Hill (R), near **Kingsbury**, where the spiritual needs of the new suburbia were met in 1933 by a Victorian church removed from Wells Street, Marylebone, and carefully transplanted here. **Queensbury** station, opened in 1934, got its name as the result of a competition run by an estate agent. Amy Johnson, who flew solo from England to Australia in 1930, learnt to fly at nearby Stag Lane aerodrome, which fell prey to developers. **Canons Park** station was named after the adjoining estate, formerly the seat of the Duke of Chandos. **Stanmore** station has the advantage of a more prominent situation than its former neighbour Stanmore Village, which was the terminus of a short LNWR branch from Harrow & Wealdstone, and from which no doubt it took considerable business. The remains of another ill-fated project, an abortive Northern Line extension from Edgware to Bushey Heath, can be found alongside Elstree Road. Commenced in 1939, work already under way was suspended for the duration of the war and never resumed.

The Stanmores (Great and Little) cover a large area to the west of the Roman Watling Street (the Edgware Road). The medieval tower of the parish church of Little Stanmore (or Whitchurch) may have caught your attention from the train, peering above the trees and rooftops due east from Canons Park station. The nave was rebuilt in 1715 to the order of the Duke of Chandos who lived at the nearby Palace of Canons (replaced with a smaller house in 1747, and now a school). The interior of the church is covered with the finest baroque paintings to be found anywhere in England, and contains an organ on which Handel played. The old village of Great Stanmore, half a mile west of the present station, seemingly passed away with the death of Stanmore Village station which closed in 1952. But among the rather hideous new buildings in The Broadway is a row of timber-framed sixteenth-century cottages – one of the longest jettied buildings in the country – and the delightful Ernest Bernays' Memorial Institute. Ernest Bernays, son of the rector of Great Stanmore, met his death by drowning in 1870 and this is his memorial – but developers want the site for a shopping centre. At the end of Church Road stands the parish church of St John the Evangelist, which was consecrated in 1850. Near the south porch the grave of W. S. Gilbert, of Gilbert and Sullivan fame, is marked by a stunning white angel. The ivy-covered ruin of the old brick church (1632–1850) hides behind the present building.

After Wembley Park on the route to Harrow and beyond, the next station is **Preston Road**. Difficult though it may be to believe, when this station opened in 1908 it stood alone amidst the leafy glades of rural Middlesex. Approaching Northwick Park, which like Preston Road is served only by slow trains, we pass over the West Coast Main and Watford local lines at the only place in Britain where two six-track railways cross. There is a splendid vista over acres of unblemished greensward to Harrow Hill, the tall slender spire of St Mary's Church soaring symbolically heavenward to end in a needle-sharp point high above the trees. **Northwick Park** serves an area which belonged to the Churchill family and was named after their Gloucestershire estate. Buses and trains come together to provide a convenient transport interchange at **Harrow-on-the-Hill**; if you are visiting the town, please turn to page 98 for further information. Just beyond the station six tracks reduce to four as Uxbridge trains take their leave (L) along a branch which opened in July 1904; the description of the journey north continues on page 94.

Although the Uxbridge branch was intended for electric trains, because some of the power supply equipment was not ready, services were worked by steam locomotives for the first six months. **West Harrow**, where the streets are named after past heads of Harrow School, intervenes before the Metropolitan tracks are joined by those of the Piccadilly Line (L) at **Rayners Lane**. During rush hours, trains from both lines run in common to Uxbridge, but otherwise Piccadilly trains terminate here. Less than two generations ago, before the advent of Harrow Garden Village, this was a bleak windswept spot in the fields of Middlesex, known to railwaymen as Pneumonia Junction. Diminutive Yeading Brook flows almost unnoticed through Roxbourne

A Metropolitan Line train bound for Baker Street leaves Harrow-on-the-Hill (*Photo:* I. McGill)

Park (L), on the way to **Eastcote**, where to avoid unproductive stops trains originally called only by request. In summer, however, it was frequently invaded by countless parties of excited children eager to enjoy a day at the Pavilion pleasure grounds, which eventually succumbed to builders in 1935. **Ruislip Manor** was also essentially rural until large-scale building took place in the thirties and indeed some idea of the early traffic potential is suggested by the fact that the only substantial intermediate station was **Ruislip**, which survives little changed, complete with a distinctive Met-style lattice footbridge. Something of an older Ruislip, centred on the thirteenth-century church of St Martin and huddled about the diminutive River Pinn, has survived the onslaught of suburbia. A mile or so north, extensive areas of woodland slope down to the shores of Ruislip Lido, a canal reservoir which provides recreational facilities in a lovely sylvan setting (buses 114 and H13).

After the train passes under the Central and Marylebone-High Wycombe lines (page 83), a spur comes alongside (L) from West Ruislip depot, and an expanse of tree-studded meadows is a reminder of a vanished rural past. Vestiges of old **Ickenham** survive in the delightful roofed pump which stands on a diminutive green by the church. **Hillingdon** station was originally styled Hillingdon (Swakeleys) in recognition of its proximity to a large Jacobean mansion designed by Sir Edward Wright, which in the early years of this century was the home of Arthur Gilbey, a noted vintner. Skirting Uxbridge Common (R), trains arrive in a few moments at the branch terminus, sole survivor of no less than four stations which have served **Uxbridge** at one time or another. High Street and Vine Street were termini of GWR branches from Denham and West Drayton respectively, and the original Met station in Belmont Road was replaced by the present town centre premises in 1938. Beyond the barrier is a unique feature – three stained-glass windows, which are especially striking when backlit by mellow sunlight.

Uxbridge has gradually metamorphosed from an important market town on the Middlesex/Buckinghamshire boundary into a modern businesslike suburban town, as proof of which its High Street now accommodates Hillingdon Civic Centre. The past has not entirely disappeared, however: there are the eighteenth-century Market House and further buildings of this period and earlier in and around High Street. The Crown Inn, also known as the Treaty House, has a particularly interesting past, for in 1645 both sides in the English Civil War met here with a view to negotiating a treaty which might end the conflict, but the attempt proved fruitless. Much later, Jacobean panelling in the 'Treaty Room' was bought by an American, who exhibited it in New York before having it installed at the Empire State Building. In 1953 it was returned to England and displayed at the Victoria and Albert Museum, and in 1959 it was restored to its rightful home at the Crown Inn.

Resuming the journey north from **Harrow-on-the-Hill**, four tracks to Moor Park are the result of work carried out between 1959 and 1962 to segregate fast and stopping trains as part of the Amersham electrification, thus only passengers on local trains will see more than a glimpse of the next four stations. **North Harrow** has obliterated the forgotten hamlet of Hooking Green, but with a final symbolic flourish of lineside graffiti near **Pinner** one becomes aware of a subtle transition which will soon transform the built-up environment into a more pastoral vista. Despite being surrounded by suburbia, Pinner village has retained much of its country charm, with timber-framed buildings and a High Street dominated by the parish church of St John the Baptist. On the Wednesday following Spring Bank Holiday the whole of Bridge Street and High Street becomes a fairground for the day. The annual Pinner Fair is still held under the terms of a royal charter granted in 1336 by Edward III. High Street is only a few yards from Pinner Metropolitan Line station. Do not be put off by the supermarket development right outside the station – an unfortunate blot on the landscape.

Northwood Hills is another station named as the result of a competition, and when it opened in 1933 it stood in splendid isolation among meadows, but before long was joined by the inevitable shopping parades and suburban housing. A wooded enclave over to the west screens Ruislip Lido and a large girder bridge carries trains over Rickmansworth Road towards **Northwood**. The steelwork for this bridge was fabricated before the war, and stored for the duration at Moor Park. Modestly affluent homes stand sedately in elegant gardens sheltered by an eastward ridge, crowned like a lion's mane by Pinner and Oxhey Woods; the change from suburbia to green belt is all but complete at **Moor Park** where the station stands in a pine-scented glade screened by trees from Sandy Lodge Golf Course (R). Moor Park mansion (open on weekdays, admission free) is a superb eighteenth-century residence built for merchant Benjamin Styles who made his fortune from the South Sea Bubble, and it now serves as a palatial 'nineteenth' for the renowned golf course which was laid out in part of the grounds when the estate was sold.

After a stretch of undulating well timbered country the train comes to a series of bridges spanning the River Colne, a former London Midland & Scottish Railway branch to Rickmansworth, and the Grand Union Canal near Watford South Junction. Here four tracks converge into two and at kilometre-post 73.2 Watford trains leave the main line, which is further described below.

Watford services veer away through Croxley Hall Wood to **Croxley** station, which has recently been refurbished and lies in a cutting below Watford Road, along which a new commuter village followed in the wake of the railway. Passing almost within a stone's throw from BR's Croxley Green terminus (R) (page 40) and crossing the Grand Union Canal and River Gade, after a further mile trains come to the Metropolitan Line station on the outskirts of **Watford**. Originally intended to terminate more conveniently in Watford's High Street, the branch, opened in 1925, in fact stopped short of the town centre near Cassiobury Park. Initially, trains were provided by both the Met and LNER, but the latter withdrew its services to Marylebone during the 1926 General Strike. Cassiobury Park mansion, seat of the Earls of Essex, disappeared in 1927, but its extensive grounds remain as a superb public park, threaded by the meandering River Gade and bisected by the Grand Union Canal whose towpath provides good walking. The park offers various sports facilities and provides a setting for many large outdoor events. Neighbouring Whippendell Woods are a splendidly tranquil haven ideal for walking and summer picnics, a riot of colour in autumn. For information about Watford please turn to page 40.

Meanwhile the main line forges on towards the Chilterns and soon, emerging from a tunnel (R) at Watford North Junction, there is a spur which once carried a short-lived shuttle service from Watford to **Rickmansworth**. From 1920 until 1961 a ten-minute stop here allowed for a change of engines, electric locomotives which hauled trains from London giving way to steam for the journey over the Chilterns. A deep, sheltered valley nearby is remarkable for its extreme temperature range, with consistently low night-time readings and where frost and below-freezing ground temperatures are frequently recorded, even during summer. Rickmansworth is a pleasant old town at the meeting of three rivers, the Colne, Chess and Gade, whose waters powered the mills which made this Hertfordshire's chief papermaking centre. There are plenty of shops and Hasing House, in the winding High Street, was, briefly, home of Quaker William Penn and his wife before they set out to found the American colony of Pennyslvania. The Colne Valley Park stretches south to Staines, and the Chess Valley Walk is a waymarked path following the river to Chesham, and which has been designed to facilitate access from adjacent Underground stations – full marks to those responsible! Hertfordshire County Council has published an excellent leaflet, which is an invaluable companion along the way.

Tree-girt embankments and cuttings yield tantalisingly brief glimpses into surrounding country as the train hurries onward; an ungainly viaduct carrying the M25 stalks menacingly out from the cool surrounding woodland on rows of spindly legs, like a huge concrete caterpillar, as we head towards **Chorley Wood**, a largely Victorian village surrounded by furze-covered commons with glorious views. Ramblers may join the Chess Valley Walk here, passing near ancient Chenies along the way. Exclusive dark-roofed homesteads snuggle luxuriously in the folds of a verdant landscape which rises and falls in gentle green eddies, like sea-swell on a lazy summer day, as the train continues towards **Chalfont & Latimer**, where familiar LRT 'bullseye' nameboards carry the additional message 'Junction for Chesham'. At the Amersham end of the platform a sign (L) indicating a line speed of 70 mph marks the fastest stretch of track on LRT.

Suburban development around the station constitutes a modern settlement, Little Chalfont; anyone intending to visit the Misbourne valley villages of Chalfont St Giles and Chalfont St Peter some three miles away might wish to consider cycling from here. The Chalfonts feature on page 86, since Gerrards Cross and Seer Green stations offer a closer rail approach. Picturesque Latimer beside the Chess has a memorial commemorating a horse which saved the life of the local squire during the South African War, and there are several other sites of interest nearby, all of them along the Chess Valley Walk which is waymarked from near the station.

Except for a very few weekday peak-period services to and from the City, Chesham branch trains depart from platform 3 and run beside the main lines to kilometre-post 83 where they diverge (R), descending in a series of sweeping curves along the hillside below Chesham Bois with enticing views across the valley of the infant Chess (R) before reaching, at the Met's furthest extremity, a convenient town centre terminus, occupying a site which was paid for by the citizens of **Chesham**. A growing Buckinghamshire town, its prosperity was founded on exploiting the Chiltern beech woods to produce furniture and brushes, but beer and boots were also made locally and watercress is still grown in the clear waters of the Chess which rise at Pednormead End. A number of older buildings remain to add variety, and the modern Elgiva entertainment centre caters for leisure functions. Walkers following the Chess path will find that it finishes at the station.

Amersham is the Met's other outpost, its station overlooking the Misbourne valley from Amersham-on-the-Hill, a community of modern housing and neat shopping parades which appeared in response to the railway. Old Amersham, now relieved of much road traffic and largely unblemished by ill-considered development, lies snugly along the valley floor. Buses stop outside the station, where there are timetable displays, or you can walk either via Station Road or more pleasantly by footpath through Rectory Woods. If you follow the road look for a tall and distinctive white house (L), in plan the form of a letter 'Y' and called High And Over. Somewhat dated now, its clinical concrete walls, flat roof and metal-framed windows still impress; it was a protest against architectural conservatism and was extremely controversial when built some sixty years ago. Amersham's long broad High Street is a glorious medley of half-timber and mellow brick, brightly illustrated signs announcing the presence of several old coaching inns. Stately St Mary's Church is worth pausing to see, and the handsome Town Hall of 1684, carried on a series of columns and surmounted by a bell tower, is a pleasing secular focal point. On 19 and 20 September the town centre pulsates with life, vibrant with the noise and excitement of an annual street fair. A field near Station Road contains a memorial erected in 1931 to seven local protestant martyrs who were burnt at the stake in the sixteenth century, a poignant reminder of the worst consequences of human intolerance.

British Rail services to Aylesbury leave from platform 1. As the train draws clear of classical Shardeloes, its white form prominent against a sylvan Chiltern backdrop, overlooks a lake (L). Once home of the Drake family, the mansion has undergone conversion into flats. As the train emerges from Weedonhill Wood (R), the last vestiges of LRT lineside equipment disappear, and Little Missenden can be seen (L), a picturesque and unspoilt village whose greatest treasure is its church, containing some marvellous thirteenth-century wall paintings. It is possible to discern Missenden Abbey (R), now a residential adult education centre but incorporating remains of an Augustinian abbey of 1133, as trains approach **Great Missenden**. Also in ruins is the old goods shed, hiding beneath a mantle of vegetation to conceal its half demolished embarrassment. Great Missenden stands near the source of the capricious Misbourne which, particularly during dry spells, is inclined to retreat beneath the chalk, an event which, according to local folklore, portends a national crisis. A narrow High Street is well endowed with attractive old buildings, including a large part-timbered structure where the Manor Court once met. Straggling Prestwood, about a mile to the east, has a monument in the form of a Maltese Cross which commemorates John Hampden (below).

Comfortable pale-washed houses are scattered across the landscape like coloured confections as the train climbs towards Dutchlands summit to breast the Wendover Gap, the distant wooded height of Halton Hill visible (R). **Wendover** is an excellent point from which to begin an exploration of the Chilterns, but do find time to see the village, with its wealth of timbered cottages and country inns, and former wind- and water-mills which have been converted to unusual dwellings. Halton House, part of an RAF camp, sends showers of exuberant pinnacles soaring like icing sugar fantasies above the trees of Haddington Hill (R) as the Chilterns recede and the train hurries on through the Vale of Aylesbury to **Stoke Mandeville**, where a small cluster of houses stand sheepishly about the station like chastised children, and Weston Turville village lingers stand-offishly a short distance away (R). Stoke Mandeville Hospital (L), once out of town, is now inextricably enmeshed in a modern red-brick double-glazed sprawl. In a few moments the single-track Princes Risborough branch (page 88) swings in (L) as we reach the outer limit of Metro-land at **Aylesbury**. Incredibly, Metropolitan trains once continued for a dozen miles more, to terminate at lonely Verney Junction, but that was long ago. Since 1966 when the town lost its main line services no regular passenger trains have operated beyond Aylesbury, effectively leaving a town of some 50,000 people isolated at the end of a branch line. Some six miles north, the Buckinghamshire Railway Centre has assembled an extensive collection of historic locomotives and rolling stock at Quainton Road station on what is now a freight-only line. From time to time, however, special passenger trains operate between Aylesbury and the centre.

Buckinghamshire's county town does not present its best face to railway travellers, having been disfigured by multi-storey car parks and an ugly assemblage of concrete blocks. However, a redeeming feature of these modern developments are the pleasant shopping environments such as Friars Square, which undoubtedly draw business from a wide catchment area. The town centre and bus station are only a short distance away, with excellent shops and a considerable legacy from the past. A Victorian clock tower dominates the Market Place, which it shares with monuments to three local figures: Benjamin Disraeli, Lord Chesham and John Hampden. The latter, a staunch Parliamentarian, is also recalled in the name of a local hostelry. He is remembered for his stand on a matter of principle against King Charles I, when he resisted the collection of ship-money. This particular form of levy had become obsolete, but the king attempted to reintroduce the tax without parliamentary authority. John Hampden initially lost his case, although judgement was later overturned by the House of Lords. The King's Head is an outstanding fifteenth-century inn which originally served as a monastery guesthouse. There are many quiet corners in the town, such as St Mary's Square and Down Parson's Fee, as well as an absorbing museum and art gallery.

HARROW-ON-THE-HILL

by Peter G. Scott

Harrow Hill rises some 250 feet above the surrounding Middlesex plain, and the spire of St Mary's Church is a landmark for miles around – look for it when approaching Harrow on the Metropolitan and Great Central lines, or after South Kenton on the North Western line from Euston. Unfortunately, the Metropolitan Line station named Harrow-on-the-Hill is not on Harrow Hill at all, but in Greenhill below its northern slopes, whilst Harow & Wealdstone station is even further distant.

Travellers on foot can climb the hill to Harrow town from the Lowlands Road exit of Harrow Met station (as it is known locally) by way of Lansdowne Road, Grove Fields and a footpath from the top of the fields to Roxborough Park, which will lead into St Mary's churchyard. Those not so energetic can take bus 258 (not Sundays) to Harrow High Street from the bus station (College Road exit from Harrow Met) or Wealdstone High Street (Harrow & Wealdstone station on the line from Euston).

In the churchyard terrace at the top of Roxborough Park there is a viewpoint with a metal indicator describing the view westwards to Windsor and beyond. Nearby is the Peachey Tomb, where the schoolboy Byron lay to compose his verse. A plaque records the 'Lines Written by Byron at This Place':

> Spot of my youth! whose hoary branches sigh,
> Swept by the breeze that fans the cloudless sky . . .
> Oh! as I trace again thy winding hill,
> Mine eyes admire, my heart adores thee still . . .

St Mary's Church has a history stretching back 900 years, and is the product of Norman, Early English, fifteenth- and sixteenth-century builders. The west door, at the foot of the tower, is the oldest part, dating from the twelfth century. Near the tower is a slate gravestone to the memory of Thomas Port, an employee of the London & Birmingham Railway Company – read the gruesome verse!

Harrow town is dominated by the buildings of Harrow School which was founded in 1572 by John Lyon, a yeoman farmer from nearby Preston. The school has provided seven British prime ministers, including Sir Winston Churchill. The original building, with additions, known as 'Old Schools', stands near the bottom of Church Hill. It contains the Old Speech Room Gallery, with its collections of paintings, water-colours and antiquities, and Harrovana – open most afternoons (not Wednesdays), admission free, telephone 081 869 1205 for details.

In the High Street stand two of Sir George Gilbert Scott's finest buildings – the School Chapel, which gives Harrow Hill its second spire, and the Vaughan Library. Visitors are not normally admitted unless accompanied by a school guide.

There was very limited space for commercial development on the Hill, so after the railways came local businesses gradually moved down to Greenhill, which has become the main shopping and commercial centre. Harrow town retains a handful of shops, some restaurants, and two public houses. The King's Head in the High Street traditionally occupies the site of Henry VIII's hunting lodge, while The Castle in West Street is the locals' pub.

But for the traffic, Harrow-on-the-Hill is a sleepy Victorian country town, yet it is only ten miles from London. Visit during term time when it comes to life with straw-boatered Harrow schoolboys; on Sundays tailcoats and striped trousers are the order of the day.

Above: Harrow School
Below: High Street, Harrow

BY UNDERGROUND TO THE COUNTRY II: EPPING, ONGAR and the HAINAULT LOOP (CENTRAL LINE)

by Ian McGill

The Central Line extends long tenuous limbs hesitantly into the rural fringes of south-west Essex, an area less appreciated, if no less interesting, than that served by the Metropolitan. Dwarfed by architecture designed for main-line rolling stock, diminutive tube trains rumble through cavernous tunnels and into vast echoing stations, the optimistic hopes of whose builders seem sometimes to have remained but an elusive dream. Forming a strategic artery through the heart of London beneath the West End and City, the Central is a line of remarkable contrasts, serving both the busiest and quietest stations on the Underground before fading to a peaceful conclusion amid the Essex countryside, where trains amble leisurely along a rural byway, through woodland heady in springtime with the scent of bluebells.

The nucleus of the Central Line, the Central London Railway, opened from Shepherd's Bush to Bank in 1901, becoming popularly known for a while as the 'Twopenny Tube' on account of the flat fare which was charged. Liverpool Street was reached in 1912 and remained the eastern terminus for over thirty years. East of Stratford, the Central mostly makes use of lines constructed by the old Great Eastern Railway (later to become part of the London & North Eastern Railway), and these are among the oldest parts of the present Underground network. Faced with increasing passenger dissatisfaction, yet reluctant to invest large sums of money in these lines, the LNER was eventually relieved at the prospect of handing over passenger traffic to London Transport, whose trains were to reach the LNER by means of two new sections of railway, mostly in tunnel, from Liverpool Street to Leyton via Stratford, and from Leytonstone to Newbury Park. However, the metamorphosis from steam to electric trains was delayed by the Second World War, and eventually completed in several stages against a changing social and political background during the years which followed.

In 1970 the Greater London Council assumed responsibility for London Transport policy and this had far-reaching effects, especially where services spilled over into adjoining counties. Nowhere were the consequences more serious than in Essex, where friction between the opposing ideologies and intransigent politicians of those authorities involved eventually resulted in imposition of 'Premium Fares'. Spiralling travel costs succeeded only in persuading customers to go elsewhere, declining patronage led to a search for economies, and some closures at the Essex end of the Central Line were seriously mooted, but the only major rationalisation to take place involved the loss of most trains between Epping and Ongar. It is hoped that a service fully restored for a twelve-month trial period in autumn 1989 will justify permanent retention.

This journey starts at Liverpool Street, but it could as easily be commenced elsewhere. The basic service pattern, varied at peak periods, provides trunk services from West Ruislip to Epping and from Ealing Broadway to Hainault (via Newbury Park), with additional trains on the busier parts of the line. Local services operate between Woodford and Hainault (but not after about 8p.m.) and from Epping to Ongar. There are no booking offices at North Weald and Ongar, but a range of tickets is available from machines which can give change. This summary is for guidance only; more detailed information may be found by consulting the free Central Line timetable booklet, or posters which are displayed at stations.

From **Liverpool Street**, eastbound trains pursue their subterranean travels below

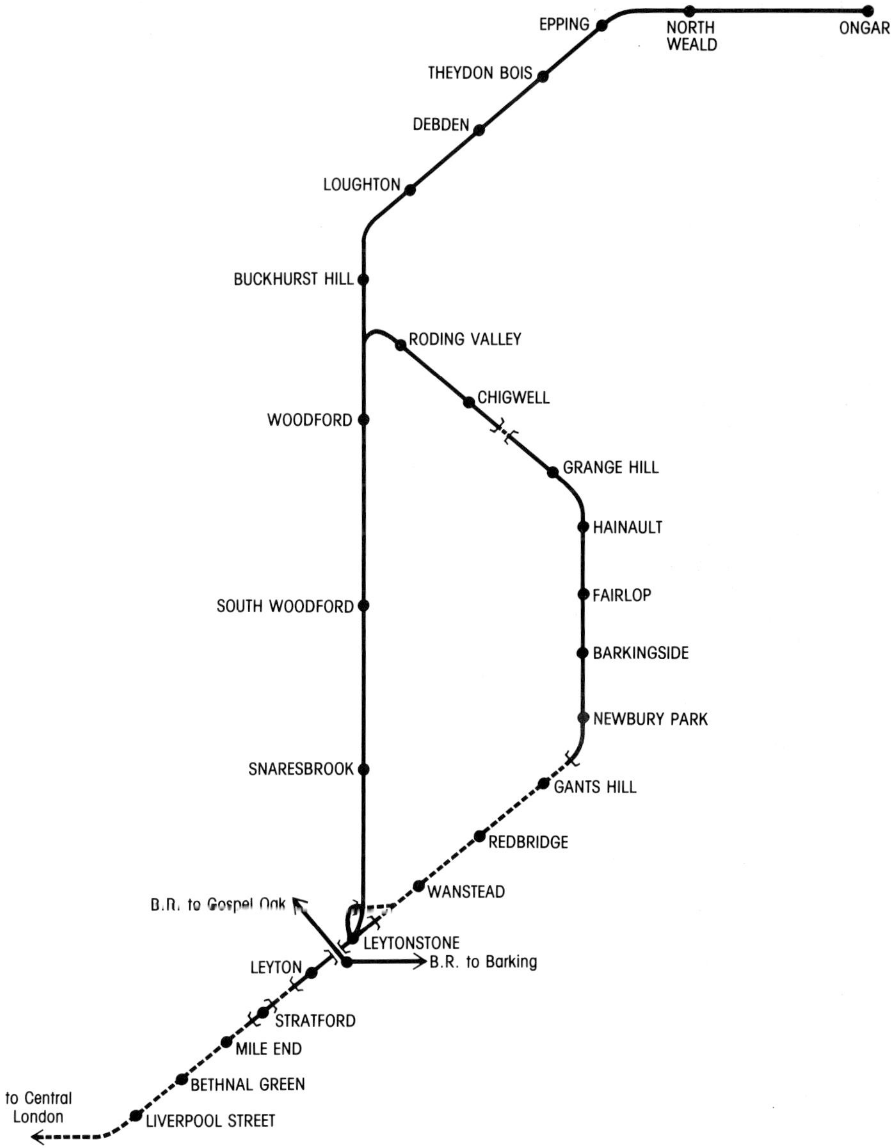

the East End in tunnels which were opened in 1946 as the first stage of the Central Line's eastward thrust. **Bethnal Green** covers an area once known as Hopetown, which was settled by French refugees fleeing from religious persecution following the Edict of Nantes. The unopened Underground station served as a public air-raid shelter during the Second World War, and was the scene of a serious incident when an accident on the stairways led to many casualties among would-be shelterers. In Cambridge Heath Road, the Museum of Childhood (tel. 081 980 2415) has an incredible collection of toys, games, doll's houses and much else including examples of Spitalfields silks, products of a defunct local industry. Housed in an impressive building which was part of the original Victoria and Albert complex at South Kensington, this museum is in fact part of the V&A. Bethnal Green BR station is about half a mile away.

Rising briefly to sub-surface level at **Mile End**, for convenient connections with District Line services, Central Line trains then burrow like energetic moles below Stratford Marshes, only to climb steeply upwards again for a brief gasp of air at **Stratford**, where connections are made with BR and Docklands Light Railway services. Plunging once more into Stygian darkness, trains descend with the urgency of a diving submarine, surfacing just short of **Leyton** station to join the former LNER, where there is a glimpse (L) of the extensive BR Temple Mills marshalling yards and the site of a junction which, after the arrival of Underground trains in 1947, allowed continued access for goods and occasional BR passenger services. Freight traffic had ceased by the mid-1960s, but a few BR passenger trains lingered on until 1970. Leyton is the home of Orient Football Club, whose name was suggested many years ago by a player employed by the Orient Shipping Line, and there is an impressive sports and leisure complex nearby at the southern end of the Lea Valley Park.

By the close of the last century development had resulted in the sea of tired streets and terraced housing which lap menacingly, like a flowing tide, on all sides. St Patrick's Cemetery (R) is a tranquil oasis where angels frozen in stone pause, arms outstretched and open-winged, while ornate multi-hued marble memorials, shining, soar aloft, proclaiming 'Nearer My God To Thee', mute testimony to the skills of monumental masons amid a forest of lesser headstones, massed in silent tribute to the departed. Quickly reasserting its dominance, as if resentful of such hallowed incursions, the urban landscape closes in around BR's Gospel Oak–Barking line which passes overhead, the platforms of Leytonstone High Road station (R) perched aloft on a viaduct wading clumsily through the mêlée of cramped thoroughfares below. At **Leytonstone** the Hainault Loop branches off; for a description of the route from Leytonstone to Epping, please see page 104.

Full of youthful enthusiasm, the Hainault Loop begins by tunnelling eastwards, but after unfulfilled adventures around the urban periphery returns weary, like a prodigal son, to be reunited with its parent near Woodford. Trains to Hainault (via Newbury Park) traverse the greater part of this loop, diverging just north of Leytonstone station, and proceeding below Eastern Avenue. Train services commenced in 1947, but the tunnels, already completed before the outbreak of war in 1939, were partly occupied as an underground factory during the hostilities.

Wanstead was once a fashionable village beside the River Roding, and enjoyed transient popularity as a spa. The beautiful parish church of St Mary the Virgin, dating from 1790, and some eighteenth-century buildings in the High Street, remain as tangible evidence from an earlier period. Look also for an inscription recording an incident which occurred on 17 July 1752 when two labourers, working in the High Street, relieved a passing trader of a cherry pie and being apprehended were fined half a guinea (52½p). Part of the manorial estate survives as Wanstead Park, a delightfully wooded enclave of almost 200 acres, featuring many flowering shrubs, and a chain of lakes with bosky islets. Beyond lies the grassy expanse of Wanstead Flats, mostly given over to sport and recreation. Both are within walking distance of the stations at Wanstead and **Redbridge.** Platforms at the latter are so near the surface that access is by means of steps, instead of the more usual escalators. Valentine's Park, another of the open spaces along the lower reaches of the Roding, is near **Gants Hill** station, whose platforms are separated by a spacious hall, its lofty arched ceiling somewhat reminiscent of the Moscow Metro. Emerging into the open once more, trains regain former LNER tracks at **Newbury Park**. Suburban growth now peters out, with the railway effectively forming the outer limit of the built-up area.

The first of three closely spaced stations is at **Barkingside**, a district so named because it lay on the edge of Barking parish. In 1750 Samuel Whitbread bought land here for the benefit of his dray horses, but nowadays the brewery sends its shires for rest and retirement to Kent. The station, a handsome structure of 1903, has some fine roof timbers visible in the booking hall, the central part of the roof is crowned by a delightful baroque cupola, and like most of its neighbours it has cast-ironwork incorporating the GER monogram, and some etched glass. From the lofty elevation of an embankment there are extensive views across Fairlop Plain (R), whose rural aspect is in stark contrast to the serried ranks of buildings, dominated by the grim grey bulk of Claybury Hospital (a former London County Council institution of 1893), which stretch in unbroken monotony to the horizon (L). Fairlop Waters Leisure Centre is adjacent to **Fairlop** station, which otherwise is somewhat isolated, nearly half a mile from the focal point of estates and shopping parades at Fulwell Cross, and was one of several candidates considered for closure by the now defunct Greater London Council. The flat expanse of Fairlop Plain served as a military airfield during both World Wars, and in the intervening years almost became London's main civil airport. A fair used to be held hereabouts beneath the Fairlop Oak, a tree of considerable proportions which was felled last century. Half a mile further on the train reaches journey's end at **Hainault**, and if, as is likely, the remaining passengers are few it is worth reflecting that in 1908, only five years after opening, receipts were so unpromising that both station and goods yard were closed and thus remained for many years.

Hainault Forest, about 1½ miles away, is like neighbouring Epping Forest a remnant of the great Forest of Waltham, itself once part of the Royal Forest of Essex. It is a pleasant spot, with waymarked walks, and may be reached by buses 150 (bound for Chigwell Row) and 247 (for Romford), which operate daily, stopping near the station in New North Road. Surprisingly, the name Hainault here does not possess a French pedigree, but is the modern form of Hyneholt, a name of Early English origin. The present spelling may be attributable to a romantic, if imaginary, connection with Philippa of Hainault, wife of King Edward III.

Between Hainault and Woodford, the north side of the loop was equipped for Automatic Train Operation in preparation for full-scale introduction on the Victoria Line. A shuttle service of local trains operates about every twenty minutes. At first the view is dominated by the huge Hainault depot, where trains are stored and serviced. Because of the exposed site, snow fences, an unusual feature in England, and since replaced by more elaborate precautions, were erected in an attempt to afford some protection against severe winter weather conditions. **Grange Hill** station, at the depot's western extremity, is the terminus for a few rush-hour trains from London via Woodford. Anyone of an energetic disposition might care to stroll 1½ miles or so, to rejoin a train at Chigwell, through a pleasant leafy locality which exudes a degree of affluence and respectability suggestive of afternoon tea and golf, swimming pools and Porsches, populated by multi-car families with little need of trains. Small wonder that this part of the Underground, once threatened with closure under the aegis of the GLC, is now something of a backwater where the service fades away to nothing by mid-evening.

Assuming a distinctly rural character, the journey is enhanced by well timbered cuttings, briefly interrupted by a short tunnel, before reaching **Chigwell**, whose long dark platforms, languishing in sylvan shade-drenched depths, are disturbed only rarely by the merest ripple of activity. William Penn was educated at Chigwell, and George Shillibeer, pioneer of London's omnibuses, is buried in the churchyard some half a mile north. The seventeenth-century King's Head Inn was used by Charles Dickens, with some artistic licence, as a basis for the Maypole Inn of his novel *Barnaby Rudge*; Chigwell Hall, the former manor house, was rebuilt in 1876 by Norman Shaw. Over towards Chigwell Row, nearly two miles away, lay the wells, a modest and long-defunct spa. Instead of retracing one's steps, it is possible to continue by way of Chigwell Lane to Debden station (below), about 1½ miles away. A long pre-stressed concrete box-girder bridge near Newbarns Farm carries trains unobtrusively over the M11 and its incessant flow of traffic. Dallying lazily, the River Roding, soon to lose its youthful rustic innocence, babbles excitedly beneath the line and onwards to eventual union with the Thames at Barking Creek. **Roding Valley** started life in 1936 as a modest halt to serve adjacent new housing estates, and is so close to Woodford Junction that from its platforms one can see trains passing on the line to Epping. In just under a mile, after negotiating the junction, the train arrives at **Woodford**, where it terminates.

Those services coming direct from **Leytonstone** have taken a shorter route along the western side of the Roding Valley, from **Snaresbrook** pursuing a course between the river the scattered fragments of Epping Forest. Suburbia's inexorable advance began almost imperceptibly, like middle-age spread, early this century, accelerating towards Loughton as homes along the forest fringe gained popularity. **South Woodford** (formerly George Lane) station is encountered before stabling sidings (R) herald the approach to **Woodford**, where trains connect for Hainault. Cranwell and Milton reputedly had links with Woodford, which today is a fusion of several communities bearing that name, including Woodford Wells, once visited for the curative properties of its spring water. Distant Claybury Hospital (R) rears intimidatingly above the surrounding rooftops, and at Woodford Junction, Roding Valley station is glimpsed (R).

As the train passes into Essex near **Buckhurst Hill** the onslaught of pre-war urbanisation begins to falter, its dying eddies lapping in frustrated desperation at the unassailable woodland around **Loughton**. Extensive sidings, here as elsewhere occupied for much of the day by empty trains, are indicative of the amount of rolling stock needed to run an intensive peak-period service on a busy urban railway. Loughton station, strikingly rebuilt in a distinctive style by the LNER, has been plagued by serious outbreaks of graffiti; in an attempt to arrest this form of vandalism LRT commissioned an attractive mural of Epping Forest which is supposedly able to resist such attempts at defacement. This is one of the few Underground stations where, paradoxically, escalators take passengers up from street level to the trains.

Clothing a ridge of high ground between the rivers Lea and Roding, Epping Forest burgeons into a luxuriant mantle of woodland hereabouts, providing shelter for a wealth of bird and plant life. Patient visitors may observe rabbits, deer and grey squirrels, but mammals such as the weasel and badger are rare. The best approach on foot is along Station Road and Forest Road, a distance of about three quarters of a mile. Once a royal hunting preserve, these remaining tracts were threatened with destruction until acquired by the City of London Corporation in 1882. Lopping Hall features a terracotta relief recalling the custom once observed on Lopping Day (11 November) each year, when local folk gathered at midnight on Staple's Hill and lit a fire in assertion of their right to cut firewood from the forest. Activities of a more nefarious nature were conducted by Dick Turpin the highwayman, who is said to haunt Trap's Hill dragging a screaming woman behind his galloping steed. Should you feel inclined to visit the grave of Sarah Martin, author of 'Old Mother Hubbard', it might, therefore, be prudent to set out from **Debden** (a modern rebuild of the former Chigwell Lane) station, which is much closer to her resting place in the old parish churchyard of St Nicholas. Loughton Hall, dating from 1878, stands adjacent, on the site of an earlier mansion designed by Inigo Jones. Debden estate, a post-war housing and industrial development, represents the final major offensive by suburbia; south beyond the M11 lies Chigwell, and ahead a large modern complex (R), where banknotes are printed, is effectively the last outpost of London. Some of its windows bulge in awe at the magnitude of such distinction.

Above: Theydon Bois (*Photo:* I. McGill)
Below: Epping Forest

Gathering speed, as if glad to have shrugged off its city shackles, the train rattles and sways along with exuberant glee. Look carefully and you may notice a pillar, almost lost among foliage and leaning drunkenly on the grassy embankment (R). This iron post, which coincides with the boundary of the Metropolitan Police area, is a survivor of many such markers erected last century around London to indicate the point at which dues became payable to the City of London on imported coal and wine leaving the capital. Introduced to assist the City Corporation make good damage caused by the Fire of London in 1666, these duties were not abolished until 1889.

An impressive concrete viaduct, clearly betraying a 1930s vintage and looking suitably ill at ease in its sylvan setting, sweeps boldly across the track at **Theydon Bois.** It replaced one of six level-crossings which were abolished in advance of railway electrification. Snuggling in the shadow of Epping Forest (which may be approached via Coppice Way) and close to the station, Theydon Bois, set pleasingly about an extensive green, proudly retains its village status. Like many East Anglian communities, it boasts a fine village sign and there are several welcoming hostelries; the Sixteen String Jack commemorates John Rann, an eighteenth-century highwayman. Older readers may recall that the village came briefly to the attention of radio listeners many years ago when the late Wilfred Pickles broadcast a programme from here in his popular *Have A Go* series. 'Theydon' indicates a place where thatch was made, and the second element of the name, suggestive of French influence, evolved from a local family name, de Bossco. Visit Hobbs Cross Farm at Theydon Garnon to see a large herd of pedigree dairy cattle and other farmstock, and how milk is produced. Youngsters can meet some of the animals, follow farm trails and enjoy the adventure playground, and their parents can call in at the farm shop for fresh produce to take home (tel. 037 881 2882). Cyclists may approach from either Epping or Theydon Bois, but there is no bus service and walkers should set out from Theydon Bois, which is about a mile away.

Fields, defiled by the M25 on its ceaseless orbit around London, billow in lazy undulations as the train bowls along past Ivychimneys hamlet (L) to reach **Epping** and the end of the longest regular journey on London's Underground, some thirty-four miles and 1½ hours after leaving West Ruislip. A market town once noted for sausages and dairy produce, Epping still hosts a weekly market. This is a useful railhead for ramblers, who may return on foot to Theydon Bois and Loughton, noting the prehistoric earthworks at Ambersbury Banks and Loughton Camp, or head east along the Essex Way towards Ongar. Reaching the town centre involves a stiff uphill walk which may, however, be avoided by boarding a bus at the station entrance.

A thin silver ribbon of steel beckons irresistibly onward, drifting like a gossamer thread on the summer air, through a jade and amber landscape for six more idyllic miles to reach the Central Line's farthest outpost at Ongar. Much of this area was to have been engulfed by post-war development, but the houses with their attendant influx of traffic never came, leaving the fields and hedgerows largely undisturbed. Instead, geriatric steam trains continued to splutter and wheeze asthmatically back and forth along this outermost limb long after electric trains reached Epping until, in 1957, advancing tube trains finally rendered the species locally extinct. Concerted opposition overcame threats of closure in 1970 and 1980 but the second reprieve was a short-lived victory, for in November 1983 all but a few rush-hour trains were withdrawn. However, last year saner counsels prevailed and like the reawakening of Sleeping Beauty the branch was once again infused with life.

Departing from platform 2 at half-hourly intervals for North Weald (hourly to Ongar), trains at once enter a different world, where tree-studded fields fall away (R) to the horizon, and spacious gardens of large villas (L) soon merge with trees which occasionally reveal glimpses of the chimney of St Margaret's Hospital (L) before completely closing ranks. Coopersale Street briefly claims attention (R) when a

An Ongar to Epping branch train near North Weald (*Photo:* I. McGill)

bridge affords us a view of the village, and then dense woodland, part of the old 'upper' forest of Epping, closes in all around. During autumn and winter, shafts of sunlight stab like translucent spears through the canopy of naked trees to bathe in pools of shining bronze the fallen leaves which carpet the forest floor, whilst in spring the air is saturated with a fragrance of bluebells, a shimmering sea of perfumed blue. Forest Glade peers from a clearing (L) as the M11 sweeps overhead, and the train forges on through the dappled light of Roughtallys Wood which eventually yields to pasture (R) and the outlying houses of North Weald Bassett appear against a belt of trees (L).

North Weald was one of the first places in Britain to suffer enemy air attack during the First World War, on 11 September, 1915. Possibly motivated by such raids, a military airfield was quickly established west of the village, but it was as a Second World War fighter station that North Weald gained prominence, playing a major part in the Battle of Britain, a role recalled by the village sign which depicts a Spitfire aircraft. A series of successful airshows were staged at North Weald from 1960 but after 1972, by which time an RAF presence had already ceased, these were transferred to Greenham Common. Now the airfield is the site of a huge Saturday market with all manner of goods for sale. The King's Head is a fine seventeenth-century timbered hostelry which was skilfully extended in 1927. North Weald had the last semaphore signals on the Underground; these were removed, and the signal-box and westbound platform taken out of use in 1970. Fields come right up to the station and a footpath leads south from the former level-crossing to Collier's Hatch and the Essex Way. Recent proposals envisage a military museum in the former goods yard, which together with a related scheme to locate a collection of historic rail and road transport exhibits at Ongar station, perhaps supplemented by a service of vintage Underground trains, could generate much needed additional traffic.

Dwarfed by the slender soaring masts of Ongar Radio Station, the train passes beneath Marconi bridge and hurries towards Ongar Park Hall (L) as if to escape being enmeshed by cables and hawsers draped like gigantic cobwebs over the surrounding fields. Established in 1920 by the Marconi Company, Ongar Wireless Telegraphy Station, now a British Telecom test site, incorporates the remains of a fort (L) built in 1899 as part of a proposed chain of defences for London which was inspired by a supposed threat of invasion. Abandoned Blake Hall station (L), closed in 1983, stands alone in the heart of rolling Essex countryside on a lane which wends its way to the A414 about a mile away. Twice during the next mile the driver sounds a warning to users of foot crossings as the train ambles pleasantly along through farmland where in later summer combine harvesters are busy gathering in the harvest. Blake Hall, a large white house glimpsed distantly (L), home of the Capel Cure family for almost 200 years, is an eighteenth-century mansion which was extensively altered last century. Part of the house served as headquarters and operations room for RAF North Weald during the last war and the operations room has recently been restored to house a museum which is open at weekends and bank holidays. The grounds, which are open Wednesdays to Sundays and bank holidays, include a tropical house with many exotic and fragrant plants, a garden centre, children's play area and a series of attractive gardens (tel. 0277 362502). It is feasible to walk or cycle from Ongar, but as it is impossible to completely avoid the treacherously busy A414 it is perhaps advisable to travel by bus 201 (currently operated by West's Coaches of Woodford Green, tel. 081 504 9741) which runs at hourly intervals each day, stopping at the station approach. Alight at Bobbingworth Turn, but take great care when crossing the busy main road where broken glass, mangled motoring trivia and buckled street furniture testify to an apparent selfish disregard for others by many drivers.

Soon the dark outline of Shelley Estate, a post-war London County Council housing development, can be seen across the meadows (L), and Ongar Wood (R) looms darkly towards Greensted. Rumbling over Cripsey Brook Viaduct, the train runs alongside a long single platform at **Ongar**, a typical country branch line terminus, from which distances on London's Underground are measured. Staggering in like an exhausted runner at the end of a race, the single track finally buries itself in a sand drag beyond which is the zero kilometre-post. A number of harmless European scorpions which colonised the old goods yard were thought to have arrived many years ago in a consignment of rail-borne imports from the continent, but there has been a recent claim that the creatures, not native to this country, may have been deliberately introduced.

There are in fact two Ongars, Chipping (signifying market) Ongar, where the railway terminates, and its smaller neighbour High Ongar. Chipping Ongar in particular is attractive, but unfortunately suffers from heavy traffic. The busy High Street presents a mixture of architectural styles, picturesque, impressive, and modern, and the town boasts a thoroughly up-to-date sports centre. A Norman motte and bailey castle survives as a moated tree-girt mound, and among notable features of the parish church, dedicated to St Martin of Tours, is a stained-glass window in memory of David Livingstone who lived in the town before starting his missionary work in Africa.

Ramblers will find that this is a good place from which to explore surrounding areas on foot, but for those less energetic, buses (some infrequent) serve neighbouring districts where villages like the Willingales (Doe and Spain), whose churches stand companionably side by side, retain a rare sense of timelessness. From Bansons Lane, beside Budworth Hall, a modest walk by a well defined track leads across fields to the world's oldest log church, a unique and beautiful building at Greensted-juxta-Ongar where great oak logs, split and set upright, form the nave walls. Inside, scorch marks made long ago by flaming torches which gave illumination can still be found.

An excellent illustrated guide book with more detailed information is available. The body of St Edmund, martyred King of East Anglia who became England's first patron saint (and a more tangible figure than his nebulous successor St George), rested here in 1013 on its way to Bury St Edmunds for reburial, having earlier been removed to the safety of Westminster Abbey to avoid periodic Danish raids on the east coast. Later additions to the fabric of this ancient building, dedicated to St Andrew, have served to enhance its appearance but sadly time has taken a heavy toll and urgent remedial work is needed. The present church register contains an entry recording the marriage of one of the Tolpuddle Martyrs; a group of Dorset farm workers, sentenced to transportation in 1834 because of their attempt to set up a trade union, they were eventually pardoned following public pressure and returning from Australia were resettled in the parish. A plaque at Tudor Cottage (formerly New House Farm), Greensted Green, recalls its associations with the Martyrs.

St Andrew's Church, Greensted–juxta–Ongar (*Photo:* I. McGill)

FURTHER INFORMATION

This may be obtained from regional tourist boards and tourist information centres. Four official boards cover the area included in this book:

London Tourist Board: 26 Grosvenor Gardens, London SW1W 0DU. Tel. 071 730 3450.

East Anglia Tourist Board: Toppesfield Hall, Hadleigh, Suffolk 1P7 7DN. Tel. 0473 822922.

South East England Tourist Board: 1 Warwick Park, Tunbridge Wells, Kent TN2 5TA. Tel. 0892 540766.

Thames & Chilterns Tourist Board: The Mount House, Witney, Oxfordshire OX8 8DZ. Tel. 0993 778800.

TOURIST INFORMATION CENTRES

Aylesbury: County Hall, Walton Street, HP20 1UA. Tel. 0296 382308.
Borehamwood: Civic Offices, Elstree Way, WD6 1WA. Tel. 081 207 2277.
Croydon: Katharine Street, CR9 1ET. Tel. 081 760 5630.
Gravesend: 10 Parrock Street, DA12 1EL. Tel. 0474 337600.
Harrow: Civic Centre, Station Road, HA1 2UH. Tel. 081 424 1103.
Hertford: The Castle, SG14 1HR. Tel. 0992 584322.
High Wycombe: 6 Cornmarket, HP11 2BW. Tel. 0494 421892.
Hitchin: Hitchin Library, Paynes Park, SG5 1EW. Tel. 0462 434738.
Kingston-upon-Thames: Wheatfield Way, KT1 2PS. Tel. 081 546 5386.
London: Clerkenwell: Heritage Centre, 35 St John's Square, EC1M 4DN. Tel. 071 250 1039.
- Greenwich: 46 Greenwich Church Street, SE10 9BL. Tel. 081 858 6376.
- Lewisham: Lewisham Library, 366 Lewisham High Street, SE13 6LG. Tel. 081 690 8325.
- Redbridge: Town Hall, High Road, IG1 1DD. Tel. 081 478 3020.
- Tower Hamlets: Mayfield House, Cambridge Heath Road, E2 9LJ. Tel. 081 980 4831.
- Tower of London: West Gate, HM Tower of London, EC3N 4AB. Tel. 071 730 3488.
- Twickenham: Twickenham Library, Garfield Road, TW1 3VS. Tel. 081 940 9125.

Luton: Grosvenor House, 45/47A Alma Street, LU1 2PL. Tel. 0582 401579.
Richmond: Old Town Hall, Whittaker Avenue, TW9 1TP. Tel. 081 940 9125.
Rickmansworth: 46 High Street, WD3 1EJ. Tel. 0923 776611.
St Albans: Town Hall, Market Place, AL3 5DJ. Tel. 0727 64511.
Southend-on-Sea: Civic Centre, Victoria Avenue, SS2 6ER. Tel. 0702 355122; High Street Precinct, SS1 1DZ. Tel. 0702 355120.
Stevenage: Central Library, Southgate, SG1 1HD. Tel. 0438 369441.
Uxbridge: Hillingdon Central Library, 14 High Street, UB8 1HD. Tel. 0895 50706.
Walton-on-Thames: Town Hall, New Zealand Avenue, KT12 1PS. Tel. 0932 228844.
Welwyn Garden City: Campus West, The Campus, AL8 6BX. Tel. 0707 332880.
Wendover: The Clock Tower, HP22 6DU. Tel. 0296 623056.
Windsor: Central Station, Thames Street, SL4 1PJ. Tel. 0753 852010.

OTHER USEFUL ADDRESSES

National Trust area offices for properties in the area of this book:

Southern: Polesden Lacey, Dorking, Surrey RH5 6BD. Tel. 0372 53401.

Kent & East Sussex: The Estate Office, Scotney Castle, Lamberhurst, Tunbridge Wells, Kent TN3 8JN. Tel. 0892 890651.

East Anglia: Blickling, Norwich, Norfolk NR11 6NF. Tel. 0263 733471.

Thames & Chilterns: Hughenden Manor, High Wycombe, Buckinghamshire HP14 4LA. Tel. 0494 28051.

Ramblers Association: 1/5 Wandsworth Road, London SW8 2LJ. Tel. 071 582 6878.

The Woodland Trust: Autumn Park, Dysart Road, Grantham, Lincolnshire NG31 6LL. Tel. 0476 74297.

The Redundant Churches Fund: St Andrew-by-the-Wardrobe, Queen Victoria Street, London EC4 5DE. Tel. 071 248 7461.

BUS SERVICES

Deregulation, which has tended to make life more difficult for bus travellers in the rest of the country, does not yet apply in London, and although various operators provide services under contract to London Regional Transport a degree of cohesion remains. This is reflected in bus/rail interchanges and the widespread provision of reliable information at bus stops. You can also telephone 071 222 1234 at any time for bus and Underground information. A comprehensive bus map and a series of very useful area bus guides can be obtained by telephoning 071 371 0247, or by writing to London Buses (A&P), Freepost, London SW1H 0YH, giving the routes or districts in which you are interested.

Elsewhere current information may be less easy to find. County councils continue to have an important role in the provision of bus services and readers are recommended to contact them initially. Most county authorities now have a public transport unit and many devote some resources to the production and distribution of timetable information; in some cases there are special telephone enquiry facilities.

Tourist information centres and branch libraries are often able to supply details of local bus services, and post offices, especially in rural areas, can sometimes help. Bus timetables are often displayed at Underground stations, and sometimes at BR stations. Underground timetable booklets include a directory of bus connections together with operators' telephone numbers.

County councils for the area covered by this book are:

Bedfordshire: County Hall, Cauldwell Street, Bedford MK42 9AP; County Council enquiry line tel. 0234 228337 (8 a.m. to 6 p.m. Monday to Friday).

Berkshire: Shire Hall, Shinfield Park, Reading RG2 9XG. Tel. 0734 875444 (8.30 a.m. to 5.45 p.m. Monday to Saturday).

Buckinghamshire: Passenger Transport Section, Elsinore House, 2nd Floor, 43 Buckingham Street, Aylesbury; enquiry line tel. 0296 382000 (9 a.m. to 5 p.m. Monday to Friday).

Essex: County Planners, Public Transport Branch, Globe House, New Street, Chelmsford CM1 1LF. Tel. 0245 352232.

Hertfordshire: Transport Co-ordination Unit, Planning & Estates Dept., County Hall, Hertford SG13 8DN. Enquiry line, Hertford: 0992 556765; Hitchin: 0462 38138; Watford: 0923 57405 (8.30 a.m. to 5.30 p.m. Monday to Friday).

Kent: Kent County Council, Sandling Block, Springfield, Maidstone ME14 2LQ. Tel. 0622 671411.

Surrey: County Hall, Penrhyn Road, Kingston-upon-Thames. Tel. 081 541 9367.

Other useful sources of information are *Doe's Bus/Rail Guide* (£4 post free), which provides nationwide information about bus links between principal non-rail-served towns and their rail heads, and *Doe's Directory of Bus Timetables and Enquiry Offices* (£2.50 post free). Both are obtainable from Barry S. Doe, AFIMA, 25 Newmorton Road, Moordown, Bournemouth, BH9 3NV.

BICYCLES

Bicycles can be taken on much of the Underground, an especially useful facility on the outer sections of the Central and Metropolitan lines. There is, however, a charge, and cycles are not allowed on moving escalators; on weekdays they can be taken only between 10 a.m. and 4 p.m. and after 7 p.m. Within these restrictions, bicycles may be taken on all sections of the Circle, District and Metropolitan lines (including the East London Line) and elsewhere on the following sections of route: Jubilee Line – Finchley Road/Stanmore; Northern Line – Edgware/Colindale, Hendon Central/Golders Green, East Finchley/High Barnet and Mill Hill East; Piccadilly Line – Barons Court/Hounslow West and Uxbridge, Oakwood/Cockfosters; Central Line – White City/West Ruislip and Ealing Broadway, Leyton/Ongar, Newbury Park/Hainault/Woodford; Bakerloo Line – north of Queen's Park only. Cycles are not permitted at all on the Victoria Line nor on BR between Finsbury Park and Moorgate or Waterloo and Bank.

Bicycles are carried free on Network SouthEast services subject to certain restrictions which mostly relate to rush-hour journeys in the direction of peak traffic flow. Elsewhere, and on InterCity and Provincial sector services, separate conditions apply and charges may be payable. For full details consult 'The Rail Travellers' Guide to Biking by Train', free from your local staffed station.

MAPS

A good map is invaluable, but a comprehensive London street atlas will often suffice, since many editions also cover adjoining areas of neighbouring counties.

The following Ordnance Survey 'Landranger' series maps at a scale of 1¼ inches to 1 mile are also useful: 166 Luton and Hertford, 167 Chelmsford and Harlow, 168 Colchester and the Blackwater area, 175 Reading and Windsor, 176 West London, 177 East London, 178 Thames Estuary.

ISBN 0-7117-0528-3

© Railway Development Society 1990
Published by Jarrold Publishing, Norwich
Printed in Great Britain 1/90